Elite • 186

Vietnam Infantry Tactics

GORDON L. ROTTMAN ILLUSTRATED BY PETER DENNIS
Series editor Martin Windrow

First published in Great Britain in 2011 by Osprey Publishing,
Midland House, West Way, Botley, Oxford, OX2 0PH, UK
44-02 23rd Street, Suite 219, Long Island City, NY 11101, USA

E-mail: info@ospreypublishing.com

© 2011 Osprey Publishing Ltd.

All rights reserved. Apart from any fair dealing for the purpose of private study, research, criticism or review, as permitted under the Copyright, Designs and Patents Act, 1988, no part of this publication may be reproduced, stored in a retrieval system, or transmitted in any form or by any means, electronic, electrical, chemical, mechanical, optical, photocopying, recording or otherwise, without the prior written permission of the copyright owner. Inquiries should be addressed to the Publishers.

Every attempt has been made by the Publisher to secure the appropriate permissions for material reproduced in this book.

If there has been any oversight we will be happy to rectify the situation and written submission should be made to the Publishers.

A CIP catalog record for this book is available from the British Library

ISBN: 978 1 84908 505 2
E-book ISBN: 978 1 84908 506 9

Editor: Martin Windrow
Page layout: Ken Vail Graphic Design, Cambridge, UK (kvgd.com)
Typeset in Sabon and Myriad Pro
Index by Margaret Vaudrey
Digital maps by JB Illustrations
Originated by PDQ Digital Media Solutions, Suffolk, UK
Printed in China through World Print Ltd.

11 12 13 14 15   10 9 8 7 6 5 4 3 2 1

Osprey Publishing is supporting the Woodland Trust, the UK's leading woodland conservation charity, by funding the dedication of trees.

ACKNOWLEDGMENTS

The author is indebted to the 1st Cavalry Division Museum, Fort Hood, Texas, for assistance with photographs.

ARTIST'S NOTE

Readers may care to note that the original paintings from which the color plates in this book were prepared are available for private sale. All reproduction copyright whatsoever is retained by the Publishers. All enquiries should be addressed to:

Peter Dennis, Fieldhead, The Park, Mansfield, Nottinghamshire NG18 2AT, UK

The Publishers regret that they can enter into no correspondence upon this matter.

Front cover: US infantry moves forward against Viet Cong positions, Dak To, South Vietnam, 1966. (US Army/ARC 530611)

Abbreviations

ACAV	armored cavalry assault vehicle
AFV	armored fighting vehicle
ANZACs	Australian/New Zealand troops
AO	Area of Operations
APC	armored personnel carrier
ARVN	Army of the Republic of Vietnam
CP	command post
CSC	Combat Support Company
CTZ	Corps Tactical Zone
FO	forward observer (artillery or mortar)
H&I	harassing and interdiction (fire)
LAW	light antitank weapon
LMG	light machine gun
LP	listening post
LZ	landing zone
MACV	Military Assistance Command, Vietnam
NVA	North Vietnamese Army
RR	Recoilless rifle
RON	remain overnight
RTO	radio-telephone operator
RVN	Republic of Vietnam (South Vietnam)
SLR	self-loading rifle (FN L1A1 rifle)
TAOR	Tactical Area of Responsibility
TO&E	Table of Organization and Equipment
VC	Viet Cong
XO	executive officer (second-in-command)

Linear measurements

Even though the metric system was employed in the former French colony of Vietnam, in this text we generally use the contemporary US system of inches, feet, yards, and statute miles. To convert these figures to metric the following conversion formulas are provided:

feet to meters	multiply feet by 0.3058
yards to meters	multiply yards by 0.9114
miles to kilometers	multiply miles by 1.6093

CONTENTS

INTRODUCTION   4
The opposing forces

TERRAIN AND CLIMATE   8
Varieties of vegetation . Roads . The impact of the "Rome plow"
Maps . Temperature and humidity

INFANTRY UNIT ORGANIZATION   12
Divisions and regiments/brigades . Battalions and companies
Rifle platoons: US Army – US Marine Corps – ARVN – Australian Task Force

INFANTRY WEAPONS   19
Rifles . Light machine guns . Grenade-launchers . Assessment

MOBILITY   25
Airmobility . Water transport . Mechanized tactics

MOVEMENT ON FOOT   28
Movement formations . Engagements . The "RON" position

FIRE SUPPORT   38
Artillery . Air support . Radio communications

SMALL-UNIT TACTICS   42
Linear and non-linear battlefields – Tactical Areas of Responsibility
"Triangular" organization . Patrols: reconnaissance – security – combat
Ambushes: layouts – getting into position – ranges – counterambush tactics – typical errors
Area-saturation operations: 2d ARVN Division, 1963 – cordon and search – search and destroy

CONCLUSIONS   62

BIBLIOGRAPHY   63

INDEX   64

VIETNAM INFANTRY TACTICS

INTRODUCTION

This book is about small-unit infantry tactics in Vietnam. While there were also mechanized infantry, armored reconnaissance, tank, and other mounted units, Vietnam was largely an infantryman's war. That being said, Free World Forces benefited from the helicopter, and airmobility proved to be essential to their operations.[1] Even if a unit was not lifted into combat by helicopters, the choppers delivered supplies, evacuated casualties, provided reconnaissance and fire support, and carried out a host of supporting missions. Even so, once on the ground the infantry faced the age-old contest of soldier against soldier, in small-unit fights in which the most basic tactical and fieldcraft skills were essential. It did not make any difference if a unit were standard "straight-leg" infantry, airborne, airmobile, dismounted mechanized, riverine ashore, Marines, ANZACs, or ARVNs: on the ground, certain basic fundamentals governed tactics – the quintessential need to "move, shoot, and communicate."

There were too many national contingents to detail all their variations on these fundamentals in a book of this size, and our primary focus will be on the tactics employed by the US Army, US Marines, and the Australian and New Zealand soldiers ("ANZACs") of 1st Australian Task Force. The tactics of the Army of the Republic of Vietnam (ARVN) and the Asian contingents were similar to those of the Americans; they were trained and advised by the US forces, and provided with US weapons and equipment.[2] There were, of course, differences; some stemmed from national preferences and scales of equipment, but they were largely due to terrain, local situations, specific missions, and efforts to find new and effective tactics in a changing battlefield environment.

The tactics employed by all the combatants were by no means fixed. They were "evolutionary," constantly changing, and differing between units – just because one unit performed an action in a particular way, it did not mean that other units did the same. Operational summaries and lessons-learned studies

---

1 The Free World Military Assistance Forces included South Vietnam's allies that contributed combat forces – the United States, Australia, New Zealand, South Korea, Thailand, and the Philippines.
2 See Osprey Battle Orders 33: *The US Army in the Vietnam War 1965–73*; BTO 19: *The US Marine Corps in the Vietnam War 1965–75*; Elite 103: *Vietnam ANZACs 1962–72*; and Men-at-Arms 458: *Army of the Republic of Vietnam 1955–75*.

During movement across country, 10-minute rest breaks were called every hour. The soldier on the left uses his elasticated helmet-camouflage band to hold minute-delay time fuses, M60 fuse igniters, and a "spoon" loading adapter that allowed 10-round stripper clips to be loaded into M16 magazines. The soldier on the right has a Claymore mine bag slung beneath his left arm, holding extra M16 magazines.

were available, but for the most part units developed and tailored their own tactics and techniques. This was not a matter of divisional doctrine – in many instances tactics even differed between companies within the same battalion. Units adapted their tactics and techniques to the terrain, weather, changing enemy tactics, their mission, and their cumulative experience. They sought new techniques to deal with changing situations and opposition, and to confuse the enemy. There were no manuals laying down rock-solid "doctrine" – unlike today, that term was seldom heard. Manuals simply

Under magnification, seven UH-1 Huey helicopters can be made out here, making an airmobile assault on a valley floor covered with rice paddies and nestled between jungle-covered ridges. Enemy fire might greet the inserted troops from any direction, or several. The platoon being landed will probably pull into the jungle on the far side of the paddies.

In dense tropical vegetation, an assistant machine gunner – identifiable by his ammo belts – makes his way down an overgrown and almost invisible trail. These belts for the M60 are carried with the bullet tips outward, so as not to dig into his neck; his lack of a helmet is unexplained.

provided guidelines, as a basis from which new tactics and techniques evolved. This "non-standardization" has been condemned, but what purpose would a more rigid approach have served? In counterinsurgencies and prolonged low-level conflicts with no definable frontlines, the constant refinement of tactics is absolutely essential.

The term "guerrilla war" is often applied to the Vietnam War. The Viet Cong (VC) local-force guerrillas played a key role, but this diminished through the course of the war. By the late 1960s, and especially after the Tet Offensive in early 1968, they were barely a military force. They continued to assist the NVA, however; they helped control rural populations and food resources in many areas, and were a persistent nuisance for Free World Forces. VC Main Force and regular NVA (North Vietnamese Army) units operated out of Laos and Cambodia – privileged sanctuaries – in their efforts to seize key South Vietnamese towns and cities and to secure areas from which to launch future operations. It must be understood that by 1968 most VC Main Force units were in fact manned by the NVA; Free World Forces had inflicted great losses in the VC ranks, while war-weariness and growing opposition to VC terrorism and oppression limited the number of sympathizers and willing recruits. These NVA and VC Main Force units were not guerrillas themselves, but light conventional forces supported by local guerrillas (who served as scouts, guides, and porters, and provided local security, food, and other supplies).

The NVA may have employed some guerrilla-like tactics and techniques, but they conducted regimental, divisional, and multi-division operations, directly attacking Free World Forces and seizing population centers. They did so without air support or tanks, employed mortars and rockets instead of tube artillery, used only light antiaircraft weapons, and had an extremely lean

A — SQUAD/SECTION MOVEMENT FORMATIONS

Full-strength squads/sections are illustrated here – US Army, ARVN and ANZAC squads, 10 men, and US Marines, 14 men – but actual field strength varied, typically between six and nine men.

The standard **US Army squad** movement formations were the column, line, "V," wedge (inverted "V"), and echelon. In Vietnam the column (**A1**) and line (**A2**) were common, the former being used for movement and the latter when engaged or moving across large open areas. An unofficial formation used by a squad conducting a patrol detached from its platoon was the "T" (**A3**), providing fire both forward and to the flanks. In this formation the trailing fire team could either move up on line with the lead team, or, if engaged from the flank, the lead team could swing into line with the trailing team. Squad-sized patrols would also use the column and line formations, and if in column the fire-team leader who was designated assistant patrol leader would bring up the rear. The pointman was a designated rifleman; he would often be followed by designated backup men, and a navigator (most likely the squad leader or a team leader). ARVN squads used similar formations, but had only one M79 grenadier. The **US Marine squad**, with three fire teams, used similar formations but modified for three teams; here we show a dispersed wedge formation (**A4**), used in open terrain. *Personnel key, US:* **1** = squad leader, **2** = fire-team leader, **3** = grenadier, **4** = riflemen.

The standard **ANZAC section** formations were termed the single file (**A5**), extended line (**A6**), staggered file (**A7**), and open file (**A8**). The single file and extended line were employed in much the same way as the US column and line. The staggered and open files were used in more open terrain, depending upon visibility. The section commander usually accompanied the gun group, while the second-in-command (2iC) ran the rifle group. The grenadier might be the 2iC or a rifleman, and could be placed anywhere in the formation; he also retained his rifle. *Personnel key, Australian*: **1** = section commander, **2** = 2ic, **3** = scout, **4** = machine-gun group, **5** = riflemen.

logistics tail. This character was shaped by the nature of the highly mobile enemy that they faced – backed by massive fire support, with superior communications and bottomless logistics, and operating from fixed bases. The country's road system was minimal, and the Free World Forces mostly controlled it – or at least, sufficiently to supply their bases. The NVA/VC were forced to travel from their sanctuaries and base areas over rough terrain, concealing their movement, and carrying everything on their backs. By contrast, the Free World Forces' domination of the sky allowed them to deploy rapidly and sustain troops by helicopter.

The NVA/VC occupied or controlled to varying degrees large portions of the country, carrying out armed attacks and imposing a reign of terror. The overriding mission of the Free World Forces in South Vietnam was to establish a secure environment free from enemy exploitation, pressure, and violence, within which it was hoped that the people could form a government that was independent, stable, and freely elected – one that would deserve and receive popular support. This was attempted by conducting aggressive combat operations focusing on NVA/VC forces, to destroy them by fire and maneuver and to disrupt their logistics.

TERRAIN AND CLIMATE

Vegetation

The jungle that covered large tracts of Vietnam was little different from temperate-zone forests. A jungle is merely a tropical forest, with the accompanying high humidity. Because of the higher moisture content than temperate forests, there is more diversity in the types of trees and other vegetation.

Some areas were described as double- and triple-canopy forest, with layered, superimposed tree canopies at different heights; because less sunlight reached the ground, such forests often had little undergrowth. Military maps identified dense and clear forests by areas of light and paler green, respectively, stating: "Dense forest or jungle indicates that more than 25 percent of ground is concealed by canopy with undergrowth generally impassable on foot.

The Central Highlands of South Vietnam was a vast region of gently rolling hills and plateaux covered with high grass and scattered clumps of trees.

Clear forest indicates that more than 25 percent of ground is concealed by canopy with undergrowth generally passable on foot." The latter would mean double- or triple-canopy. This classification was made by studying aerial photographs, and was not entirely accurate. The Army's contention was that there is no such thing as actually impassable terrain; infantry could pass through virtually anything, albeit slowly – in densely overgrown terrain, progress might be only 400–500 yards per hour. Land navigation was difficult in dense vegetation, where it was almost impossible for a unit to pinpoint its location to call for fire- and air support; even nearby landmarks could not be seen, to confirm one's location on the map. In such forests it was impossible for aircraft to detect the enemy, who often did not even halt their movement when aircraft were overhead.

The terrain of South Vietnam ranged from the mountainous north, interspersed with winding valleys, down through the rolling hills and plateaux of the Central Highlands, the triple- and double-canopy forests further south, to the sprawling river- and canal-cut marshes of the Mekong Delta. Within all of these regions troops might find themselves among hills, ridges, gullies, ravines, swamps, forests, large areas covered with bamboo thickets, and vast expanses of man-high elephant grass or brush, greatly hampering movement on foot. The bamboo and grass were so tall and dense that navigation was just as difficult as in jungles. A man did not walk *through* dense elephant grass; he had to walk *over* it, pushing it down (and leaving a distinct trail). Intermingled brush and snagging "wait-a-minute" vines made this even more difficult. Trackless bamboo thickets, with scattered trees, could cover huge areas; they were extremely difficult to negotiate, sometimes actually forcing troops to crawl. There were also broad areas of cultivated rubber-tree plantations; unless abandoned, these were park-like, devoid of undergrowth and crisscrossed with a road-grid. The trees were planted in straight, uniformly spaced rows, their crowns growing together so densely that aircraft could not see the ground, nor could ground troops see aircraft.

In thick vegetation the soldier had to move quietly, and minimize the movement of foliage that would signal his presence. He had to listen for sounds that might warn him of the enemy – striving to distinguish them through the background jungle sounds, the inevitable noise of the unit's own movement, overhead helicopters, distant artillery, and so on. At other moments the jungle might be eerily quiet, with not a sound to be heard. Visibility was often short-ranged, but in most instances a soldier could see two to four of his comrades when deployed on line, and more of his unit were often visible. Some 20–30 yards of relatively unobstructed visibility was common, and sometimes more, and a man might suddenly come upon areas with little or no underbrush.

Regardless of the short visual distances, the enemy were difficult to detect. Vegetation was layered, and one had to learn to look through each layer to detect

A corporal section commander (note the M16 rifle) from 2nd Bn, Royal Australian Regiment photographed in 1967 in the park-like terrain of a rubber-tree plantation. With a TAOR measuring 38 × 18 miles, the 1st Australian Task Force in Phuoc Tuy Province eventually comprised two infantry battalions, an artillery regiment, an APC squadron, a tank squadron, a Special Air Service squadron, and service support elements. The Australian and New Zealand infantry pursued a doctrine of nonstop patrolling from their Nui Dat base camp, staying out for long periods and aiming to dominate the countryside. (Photo Australian War Memorial, Canberra)

It was not only the mighty "Rome plow" that played an important role in supporting infantry operations, by clearing fields of fire and destroying enemy hiding-places. Here a light helicopter-transportable bulldozer is used by an airmobile or airborne unit to make a "tactical cut," clearing the brush around a firebase.

some shape, movement, or color that did not fit the jungle's texture. Light and shadows crisscrossed and changed. Movement demanded constant vigilance and awareness; letting down one's guard at the wrong moment could be fatal. More than anything else, it was movement that alerted one to the enemy's presence, but listening was just as important.

Roads

The country's road system was undeveloped. There were National (*Quoc lo* – QL) and Interprovincial (*Lien tinh lo* – LTL) routes, most of which were two-lane asphalt and banked up above ground level to improve drainage. Provincial (*Tinh lo* – TL), and communal (*Huong lo* – number only) routes were packed- or loose-surface dirt roads, usually unbanked. Their condition depended on how much Free World Forces relied on them and made efforts to maintain them. In remote and contested areas they deteriorated badly with the seasonal rains. On many roads the VC had long since blown up every bridge and culvert, and they remained unrepaired unless major military operations took place in the area. In many areas the countryside was laced with one-lane dirt roads, cart tracks, and footpaths. Maps might show many of these, but they could not be relied upon; many were overgrown owing to long disuse, and newer trails might have been created. In the Mekong Delta there were even fewer roads, as the main transport routes were the 1,500 miles of rivers and 2,500 miles of man-made canals.

A peculiarity of the Vietnam War was the "Rome plow," and the impact it had on terrain and tactics. So named after the Rome Plow Company of Rome, Georgia, this was a Caterpillar D7E bulldozer fitted with a massive tree-slashing blade. Echeloned lines of dozers would grind through the forests, taking down trees. Rome plows employed three types of "cuts." "Area cuts" saw the leveling of broad swathes of jungle in areas containing enemy base camps, supply caches, defensive positions, and tunnel complexes. Such activity would flush the enemy out, so required security forces to protect the dozers, and maneuver forces to pursue the fleeing enemy and react to counterattacks. These cleared areas and wide-cut lanes might be sown with remote sensors to detect movement, and ambush patrols and aircraft would keep what was known simply as "a Rome plow" – the cleared swathe – under surveillance. "Road cuts" cleared bands 100–300 yards wide on either side of lines of communications, in order to keep ambushers at a distance and make the laying of command-detonated mine wires difficult. This was undertaken on roads important for convoys supplying bases, as well to safeguard commercial traffic. "Tactical cuts" cleared sites for firebases and landing zones, and leveled fields of fire around bases and villages.

Maps

The accuracy of available maps varied. Those covering more populated and accessible areas with extensive road systems were usually reliable, but the more remote and inaccessible an area, the less accurate the maps. There were claims that entire hill masses were incorrectly depicted; this was true in remote cases, but more often it was simply due to the inability to correctly determine their

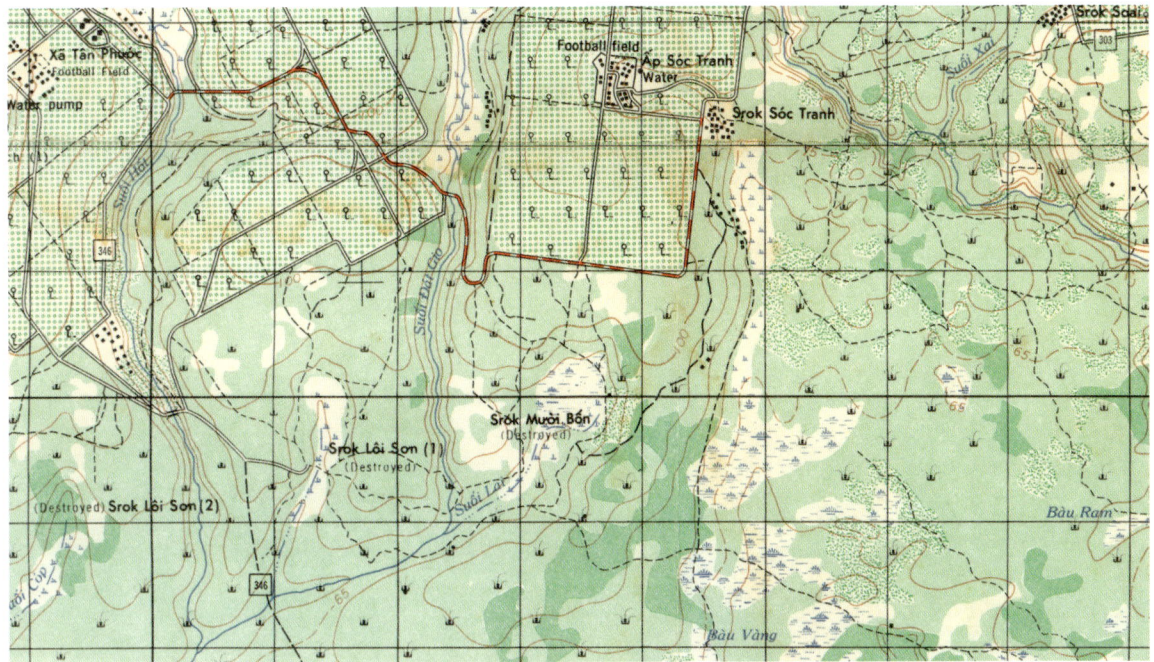

position because of dense vegetation and rough terrain. US-published maps were based on pre-World War II French surveys, and were updated from aerial photographs. If one was near rivers or major streams the maps were more accurate, since the French ran survey lines along streams as their baselines. Updated "pictomaps" were also available for highly contested areas. These were full-color aerial photographs printed as map sheets, and overprinted with topographic map symbols as on standard maps (roads, bridges, built-up areas, etc), as well as terrain contour lines and grid lines. While the areas were photographed on clear days, sometimes cloud patches obscured small areas. Standard tactical maps were 1:50,000 scale with a 1,000-meter military grid coordinate system (2cm grid squares – 0.78 inch), covering a 27 × 27km area (16.77 miles square).

Temperature and humidity

The climate had just as much effect on small-unit tactics as the terrain. It was hot, humid, and either too dry or too wet. There always seemed to be either insufficient water for drinking, or too much, causing immersion-foot or other problems. This depended on the cycle of the dry or northeast monsoon season, from November to April, and the wet or southwest monsoon from June to October. Soldiers claimed that there were three seasons – wet, dry, and dusty, occurring at hourly intervals. Heat exhaustion was something that could affect even the well-acclimatized, and hospitals complained that most wounded required extensive rehydration. Mosquitoes, jungle and water leeches, ants, swarming bees, scorpions, centipedes, poisonous snakes, and flies were troublesome. Malaria, dengue fever, dysentery, diarrhoea, and "undiagnozed fevers" were common ailments. Stories of snake and tiger attacks were more often than not just that – stories.

Daytime temperatures typically varied from the mid-80s°F to the high 90s°F (29°–36°C), with humidity around 80–90 percent. Temperatures might drop into the low 70s°F range (21°–23°C) at night, but the seasonal rains did little to lower

This section of a 1:50,000 scale topographic map – the scale used by units below division level – provides indications of different vegetation. The darker green shade indicates forest with underbrush, while lighter green areas are generally clear of undergrowth or have only light brush. Light green areas with black symbols indicate bamboo. At top and left, the densely green-spotted areas with black "lollipop" symbols are rubber plantations. The small white areas with blue symbols indicate swamps, which might be dry in the dry season. The narrow white streak running south from the village of Srok Sóc Tranh at upper right center is a rice paddy; under magnification, the "rice" symbols differ from "swamp" symbols. The three villages at lower left and center are marked "Destroyed."

temperatures. In the northern mountains the temperatures were cooler at night. Fog was experienced in the mountains, affecting air support, and sometimes occurred in other areas in the morning hours. Monsoon rains also hampered aerial operations, but had one benefit: for weeks at a time the daily rains often occurred at predictable times, allowing units to plan around the expected daily downpour, even though it would begin and end without warning.

The brutal climate was aggravated by a diet of C-rations and infrequent B-ration hot meals; by long hours of "busting brush"; by lack of sleep because of 50-percent alert (one man off, one on, at two-hour intervals); by daily stress, and the need for perpetual alertness, even when no contact was made.

INFANTRY UNIT ORGANIZATION

While this study focuses on small-unit tactics, a basic understanding of unit organization is important. Divisions – US Army and Marine, and ARVN – were basically the same organizationally. They had three infantry regiments ("brigades" in the US Army), each of three battalions; division artillery of three to four battalions; combat support battalions or companies, to include reconnaissance, engineer, and signal; and service support units such as maintenance, supply, and medical.

Free World regiments/brigades typically had three maneuver battalions, which could be cross-attached between regiments/brigades, with no or minimal support units. From 1966 most ARVN regiments had four battalions; this was reduced to three in 1971, with the disbanded fourth unit providing a fourth company to each of the other battalions. Any support was usually temporarily attached from division. US separate combined-arms brigades contained an artillery battalion, service support battalion, and reconnaissance and engineer companies; in effect, they possessed the units typically attached to a divisional brigade from its parent division. US divisions with nine to 11 maneuver battalions and significant artillery and combat support units could influence the battle, and could shift forces to support

Infantry pass through a Vietnamese village. It was often extremely difficult for troops to determine their location in jungle areas, but streams and villages were accurately located, and even destroyed villages were marked on maps as locating aids. The left man here is armed with a 5.56mm XM177E2 submachine gun, and is probably a platoon leader.

A hasty battalion command post in operation – this is a temporary affair, set up on a firebase under construction. Contact is maintained with its companies in the field, its rear support element, supporting artillery and helicopters, and the brigade headquarters. In the foreground is an AN/VRC-46 radio.

engaged units. One would think a separate brigade with three or four maneuver battalions would have one-third the combat power of a division, but it did not; it lacked the assets common to a division with which to reinforce multiple engaged units.

The battalion was the predominant fire-and-maneuver unit. It typically had a headquarters company with minimal staff, communications, supply, service, and medical elements. It might also possess combat support platoons with mortars, recoilless rifles, scouts, etc., or these combat support elements might be assigned to a separate company, as in the US and Australian armies. A US combat support company consisted of a reconnaissance (3 × 10-man squads), a mortar (4 × 81mm), and an antitank (4 × 106mm RR) platoon. The Australian support company possessed 32-man assault pioneer (demolitions, mine-clearing), mortar (6 × 81mm), antitank, and signals platoons. From late 1966 the ANZAC antitank platoon was converted to a 31-man reconnaissance platoon, divided into three sections and operating in patrols of four to six men.

Three rifle companies were the standard in most armies, although the US Marines and Australians were exceptions, with four companies from the beginning. Some Australian battalions had a fifth New Zealand company attached, mainly for security. The traditional three-company battalion was effective in conventional linear operations, but in Vietnam more flexibility was needed; four rifle companies allowed three to be deployed in the field while the fourth secured the firebase. It was not uncommon for a battalion to be tasked with both securing its base and local villages,

A platoon leader flashes a Mk III signal mirror at a helicopter to mark his location. He is probably talking to the helicopter, and using the clockface system to pass his location in relation to the aircraft's direction of flight. Mirrors were better than colored smoke grenades, since the latter could reveal the unit's location to the enemy.

and maintaining a reaction force for foot or airmobile insertion. This option saw two companies tied up on security or other missions, while still able to put two companies in the field. The fourth company would be rotated to the field just like the others – it was not tasked solely with base security. The scout platoon often operated as a separate entity, but would not often stray too far from a supporting company – a small platoon hit by an enemy company was extremely vulnerable.

In late 1967, US Army infantry and airborne battalions received a fourth rifle company plus a combat support company, but mechanized battalions did not. Airmobile and light infantry battalions already had combat support companies, and in 1967 received a fourth company. The new TO&E basically transformed the standard infantry battalion to light infantry, reducing heavy weapons and other equipment to what was necessary in Vietnam. ARVN infantry battalions had fourth rifle companies prior to 1960 (when they were withdrawn to become separate Ranger companies), but in 1971 again received a fourth company.

Rifle companies generally had a small headquarters, three rifle platoons, and a weapons platoon. In practice the weapons platoon was usually deleted and its crew-served weapons were shifted to battalion, with some placed in storage. The heavy weapons and ammunition were too heavy, and slowed the unit even if they could be man-packed. There were always exceptions, however; the NVA/VC were forced to man-pack crew-served weapons.

A soldier linking 2½lb M5A1 C4 demolition charges with detonating cord. These will be used to blast down trees to clear a helicopter landing zone, either for a routine resupply or to extract the unit.

B: PLATOON MOVEMENT FORMATIONS

Because of the often close, wooded terrain, platoons typically moved in column formation, and in line for crossing open areas and in the assault. Most platoons had three squads, but might have only two if severely understrength. Ideally, rather than conducting an assault with the whole platoon on line, the separate squads would use fire-and-maneuver, alternating bounds forward with delivering covering fire for one another. The platoon's two or three machine guns provided covering and suppressive fire, whether as part of the squads or under platoon control. Few Army units had a machine-gun squad, and the M60s were usually assigned or attached to the squads. Marine platoons usually had a two-gun squad attached from the company weapons platoon. Each ANZAC section had an integral M60. Like squads, platoons used the column (**B1**), line (**B2**), "V" (**B3**), wedge (**B4**), and echelon (**B5**) formations.

The platoon wedge formation was effective in open or sparsely wooded terrain where squads could remain in visual contact. The individual squads within the platoon might be moving in a different formation: for example, the squads within a platoon wedge formation might themselves be in column, line, or wedge. In (**B4**) the squads of the platoon are in column formation, which was good for countering an ambush; if engaged from the front, either or both of the trailing squads could maneuver to the front or envelop the enemy's flanks. The lead squad's point element (**1**) might be slightly further forward of the rest of the squad. The platoon command group follows the lead squad. It consists of the platoon leader (**2**); his RTO (**3**); a mortar/artillery forward observer (**4**) – who might have his own RTO, or might carry the radio himself; and the medic (**5**). The platoon sergeant (**6**) might follow the flanking squad on the most vulnerable flank, or might rove around the formation ensuring that the men kept their positions and that there were no stragglers. This platoon's two machine guns are attached to the flanking squads (**7**). Machine guns were never positioned with the point, in case the pointmen became casualties, and the squad had to fall back leaving the MG behind. Flank security is provided here by pairs of men from the flanking squads (**8**), who remain in visual contact with their squads. Squad leaders (**9**) typically followed either the pointman or the lead fire team.

Regardless of the formation the company moved in, when pausing for a halt each platoon would send out a team-sized patrol to either flank to conduct a "cloverleaf search" (**B6**). The patrols would loop out for a few hundred yards, paying particular attention to dense vegetation, gullies, streams, and other potential hiding-places. The tail-end platoon would send a cloverleaf patrol to the rear, or establish a stay-behind squad ambush (**B7**) for the duration of the halt.

Helicopters were essential to the infantry for support of every kind – including performing the very last service they could. Here the poncho-wrapped body of a US soldier is recovered for evacuation by a UH-1H Huey.

Rifle platoons

Rifle platoons were led by a lieutenant and a senior NCO in the headquarters, with a radio operator. There were three rifle squads (but in some cases only two, if manpower was low). Squads could range from six to 13 men, and usually numbered somewhere in between. There might be a weapons squad, usually with one or two machine guns; alternatively, these guns might be part of the platoon headquarters, or be integrated into the rifle squads. The three-platoon, three-squad structure was well suited for small-unit operations; the third squad never served as a "reserve," but was in the line.

US Army Regardless of the type of company, rifle platoons were similarly armed and organized, with an official strength of 44 men. The platoon headquarters had the platoon commander, platoon sergeant, and a radio-telephone operator (RTO). The three 10-man rifle squads each consisted of a squad leader and two fire teams (Alpha and Bravo), each with a team leader, an automatic rifleman (M14A1 automatic rifle), and a grenadier, with one team having two riflemen and the other a single rifleman. All rifle squad members were armed with rifles except the grenadiers, who carried an M79 launcher and a pistol. The 11-man weapons squad had a leader, two machine gunners and assistants, two antitank gunners and assistants, and two ammunition bearers. Antitank and machine gunners and assistants carried pistols, while the weapons squad leader and ammunition bearers had rifles. There were two M60 machine guns and two 90mm M67 recoilless rifles, or in some cases 3.5in bazookas.

All the foregoing is according to "the book" – the TO&Es – but the reality was much different. When units deployed to Vietnam they were organized and armed according to the TO&E, but with combat losses, illness, personnel detailed to firebase duties and on R&R, and slow replacement flow, platoon strength declined. The employment of weapons changed greatly. The 90mm RRs and bazookas were seldom carried to the field, and were normally placed in storage, though there were instances when one per platoon might be carried, or even just one in the company. After the issue of the M16A1 rifle there were no longer any squad automatic riflemen. These became riflemen, as did the antitank gunners, their assistants, and both ammunition bearers; assistant machine gunners also generally drew rifles.

Actual platoon strength was typically 20 to 30 men organized into two or three squads. The fire team concept was often abandoned, and the weapons squad usually ceased to exist. The two M60s were either assigned directly to rifle squads, sometimes with a third added, or to the platoon headquarters. Rifle squads often had only five to eight men. Other platoons retained four squads – three five- or six-man rifle squads, and a seven-man weapons squad with two M60s. Some platoons fielded just two rifle squads with six to eight men, but a full 11-man weapons squad with two M60s and a few riflemen. It was not uncommon for only two squads to be organized, in order to provide a higher squad strength of nine to 12 men including an organic two-man machine-gun crew.

Some squads were organized into a "point team" with a pointman, a grenadier and two riflemen, and a "gun team" with an M60 gunner and assistant, four or five riflemen, plus the squad leader. Two grenadiers were usually retained, but some small squads had only one so as not to reduce rifle strength. Often, when only two squads were employed, and because of the inexperience of some squad leaders, the platoon leader and platoon sergeant would each take charge of a squad when engaged. The medic became a fixture in the platoon headquarters, and there was usually an artillery/mortar forward observer (FO).

On paper, the rifle company had a weapons platoon with a mortar section (3 × 81mm) and an antitank section (2 × jeep-mounted 106mm RR). It was typically dissolved, with some of the weapons used for base defense. Occasionally some companies retained a mortar or two, to be used when necessary. Sometimes 81mm mortars, ammunition, and crew were airmobiled into a night location in dangerous situations, and lifted out in the morning when the company moved out. US airmobile and light infantry battalions had only a mortar platoon, lacking the recoilless rifles.

US Marine Corps The standard 44-man Marine platoon had a headquarters with a commander, platoon sergeant, and two or three messengers, one of whom was an RTO. A Navy medical corpsman and a mortar FO were attached. The three rifle squads each had 14 men: a squad leader, a grenadier, and three fire teams each with a team leader, an automatic rifleman, and two scout-riflemen. As in the Army, with the advent of the M16 the automatic

Only three Army and two Marine tank battalions operated in Vietnam, but they were not the only units to possess tanks – some of the armored cavalry squadrons also had some. Here M48A3 tanks mounting 90mm main guns cover infantry as they cross a broad, open area.

A scout dog-handler breaks from the brush, followed by an M79-armed grenadier. Each infantry brigade had an attached scout dog platoon, and each of the platoon's 24 dog teams – each of a German Shepherd and its handler – was typically attached to a rifle company. They were not always available, however, owing to team rest cycles; the dogs lacked stamina in the harsh climate.

rifleman became a rifleman. Understrength platoons might have two fire teams per squad, or two squads each with two or three fire teams.

There was no weapons squad, but the company weapons platoon (which the Marines maintained, unlike the Army) had machine gun (6 × M60), assault (6 × 3.5in bazooka), and mortar (3 × 60mm) sections. Sometimes the bazookas were placed in storage, but often at least some were retained for bunker-busting, and could be attached to rifle platoons. The M60s were organized into three eight-man squads of two guns each, with two gunners, two assistants, and four ammunition bearers (though usually fewer). The gun squads could be attached to rifle platoons or might operate under central control. Usually fewer mortars, if any, were carried in the field.

ARVN The rifle platoon officially had 33 men, but somewhere between 20 and 30 was common. The headquarters had the platoon commander and sergeant plus an RTO. The three typically 10-man rifle squads each included a squad leader, Browning Automatic Rifle man, and two four-man fire teams, though fire teams were seldom actually used. With the issue of M16s from 1968, the BAR-man became an M79 grenadier. The company weapons platoon had two M1919A6 or M60 machine guns, two 60mm M19 mortars, and two 3.5in bazookas, organized into two-squad sections.

Australian Task Force The platoon strength was officially 32 men, but 20 to 24 was common in the field. The platoon headquarters consisted of the platoon commander and second-in-command (2iC, platoon sergeant) plus two radio operators/orderlies ("Sigs"). Two radios were carried, one as a backup which stayed with the 2iC, or was carried by a detached section on patrol. The three 10-man sections (equivalent to US squads) each had a section leader and three groups: scout group, of two scouts armed with submachine guns or M16s; gun group, under the section 2iC, with a two-man M60 crew; and rifle group, directly overseen by the section leader, with up to four riflemen with L1A1 FN rifles. Either the section 2iC or a rifleman carried an M79 grenade launcher, but unlike US practice whoever carried this "wombat gun" also retained his rifle. Later, some units received XM148 or XM203 grenade-launchers mounted on M16s. Medics, stretcher bearers, a sapper for demolition work, and mortar or artillery FO parties might be attached as required. There was no company weapons platoon.

INFANTRY WEAPONS

It was necessary for infantrymen in Vietnam to carry sufficient rations, water, ammunition, and other gear over rough terrain to maintain them for several days. Free World Forces either carried all the supplies they needed for the duration of an operation – up to six days – or were resupplied by helicopter. Consequently, infantry weapons and their ammunition needed to be light, easy to operate, and reliable in an environment of dust, mud, rain, and heat, often with inadequate opportunities for cleaning. The soldier's basic ammunition load was double the standard amount or even more, since timely helicopter resupply could not always be guaranteed. It was not uncommon for one side in a jungle firefight to break contact not for tactical reasons, but simply because they were running low on ammunition.

In most areas of Vietnam the long effective range normally desired of weapons was not a factor, since visibility was extremely limited due to brush, elephant grass, and stands of bamboo. There were some areas, such as the Central Plateau and the Mekong Delta, where longer ranges were useful, but even there short-range engagements were the norm.

Free World infantry were provided generous numbers of crew-served weapons, but they and sufficient quantities of their ammunition were too heavy to man-pack in the field. There was little need for antitank weapons, so these were usually placed in storage or used for firebase defense, though a company might carry one such weapon for attacking bunkers. The single-shot disposable M72 light antitank weapon (LAW) was light and compact, and these were carried for bunker-busting and even for counter-sniper fire. Mortars were very heavy, as was the substantial ammunition supply needed if they were to be effective, and in forested areas there were few sites in which to set them up. Free World Forces always operated within range of friendly artillery; this was responsive and accurate enough to negate the need for mortars, and was further backed up by attack helicopters and close air support (CAS).

The most important infantry weapons were the individual rifle, automatic rifle, light machine gun, and grenade-launcher. These basic arms had a high impact on small-unit tactics, techniques, and performance, so are worth examining in some detail.

Rifles

The standard US rifle in 1965 was the 7.62mm M14, a heavy semi-automatic with a 20-round magazine; however, only the 1st and 25th Infantry Divisions deployed with them – in late 1965 and early 1966,

US Army & Marine infantry battalion weapons
.45cal M1911A1 pistol (Colt)
7.62mm M14 rifle
7.62mm M14(M) & M14A1* automatic rifles
7.62mm XM21 sniper rifle*
7.62mm M40 sniper rifle (Remington)†
.30cal Model 70 sniper rifle (Winchester)†
5.56mm M16 & M16A1 rifles
7.62mm M60 machine gun
.50cal M2 machine gun (Browning)
40mm M79, XM148* & M203* grenade launchers
66mm M72 & M72A1 light antitank weapons (LAW)
3.5in M20A1B1 rocket launcher ("bazooka")
90mm M67 recoilless rifle*
106mm M40A1 & M40A2 recoilless rifles
60mm M19 mortar†
81mm M29 & M29A1 mortars
4.2in M30 mortar
Notes: * Not used by the Marine Corps   † Used only by the Marine Corps

ARVN infantry battalion weapons
.45cal M1911A1 pistol (Colt)
.45cal M1A1 submachine gun (Thompson)
.30cal M1 & M2 carbines
.30cal M1 rifle (Garand)
5.56mm M16A1 rifle
.30cal M1918A2 automatic rifle (Browning)
.30cal M1919A4 & M1919A6 machine guns (Browning)
7.62mm M60 machine gun
.50cal M2 machine gun (Browning)
40mm M79 grenade launcher
66mm M72 & M72A1 light antitank weapons (LAW)
3.5in M20A1B1 rocket launcher ("bazooka")
57mm M18A1 recoilless rifle
75mm M20 recoilless rifle
90mm M67 recoilless rifle
106mm M40A1 & M40A2 recoilless rifles
60mm M2 & M19 mortars
81mm M1, M29 & M29A1 mortars

Infantrymen return fire with 5.56mm M16A1 rifles, using their rucksacks as cover. Note the bullethole in the rifle's plastic and aluminum forearm.

respectively – as did the 1st and 3d Marine Divisions. The first units to arrive in 1965 – 1s Cavalry Division; 1st Brigade, 101st Airborne Division; and 173d Airborne Brigade – deployed with 5.56mm M16 selective-fire rifles with 20-round magazines, as did all subsequent formations. The M14 was heavy, but achieved good penetration through vegetation – unlike the M16 "black rifle." The lighter M16 allowed more ammunition to be carried, a valuable feature; on the other hand, it demanded meticulous cleaning, and this and early mechanical flaws caused problems. Its full-automatic capability was not that much of a benefit, often leading to a waste of ammunition, but was useful to pointmen and in close-range ambushes.

The ARVN used the .30cal M1 Garand semi-automatic rifle. This eight-round rifle was far too heavy and awkward for Vietnamese, and could not stand up to enemy weapons with higher-capacity magazines. Many ARVN were armed with .30cal M2 selective-fire carbines, with 30-round magazines. They were light, compact, and handy in the jungle, but the weak .30 carbine round – much smaller than the .30cal used in other US weapons – performed poorly in dense vegetation, had inadequate knockdown power, and was short-ranged. Beginning in late 1966, selected ARVN units began to receive the M16A1, and this was gradually extended to all combat units into 1968.

The ANZACs of the Australian and New Zealand contingents mainly carried the 7.62mm L1A1 self-loading rifle ("SLR" – the Belgian FN-FAL design). This was a long, heavy weapon with similar characteristics to the M14 – semi-automatic, with a 20-round magazine. They began receiving some M16s in 1966, not as replacements for the SLR but rather for their 9mm Owen and F1 submachine guns. These weapons, including the M16s, were carried by officers, support troops, and section scouts. The ANZACs were quite pleased with the penetrating capabilities of the SLR, despite the drawbacks of its weight and length (though their SAS sometimes cut them down).

The NVA were armed with the 7.62mm AK-47 or AKM, a selective-fire assault rifle excellent for jungle warfare, though a bit on the heavy side. It achieved very good penetration through foliage, and the 30-round magazine increased its firepower. Prior to 1967 they mainly used the 7.62mm SKS semi-automatic carbine with a 10-round magazine; as the AK became available in quantity, the SKS was passed on to the VC.

Australian & New Zealand infantry battalion weapons
Canadian 9mm L9A1 pistol (FN-Browning)
Australian 9mm Mk 2 submachine gun (Owen)
Australian 9mm F1 submachine gun
US 5.56mm M16 & M16A1 rifles
British 7.62mm L1A1 rifle (FN-FAL)
British 7.62mm Model 82 sniper rifle (Parker-Hale)
US 7.62mm M60 machine gun
US 40mm M79, XM148 & XM203 grenade launchers
US 66mm M72 & M72A1 light antitank weapons (LAW)
British 81mm L16A1 mortar
US 90mm M67 recoilless rifle
US 3.5in M20 Mk II (M20A1B1) rocket launcher ("bazooka")

Light machine guns

Squad and platoon light machine guns (LMGs) – bipod-mounted automatic rifle-caliber weapons – were invaluable. They provided a base of fire for the maneuvering riflemen; they laid down streams of fire in the defense (and were essential for base defense); they offered longer-range fire when needed to make up for the rifles' shorter range, and could better penetrate cover materials. Ideally, each squad possessed one or two LMGs. The US Army initially used the 7.62mm M14A1, a much modified M14 rifle for the automatic rifle role, at a scale of two per squad; the Marines used the M14(M), simply a selective-fire M14 with a bipod, issued three per squad. Both were extremely inaccurate weapons.

7.62mm M60 machine-gun team lying in readiness during a rest halt; the assistant gunner is to the left. The M60 weighs 23lb, and a typical ammo load was 600–800 rounds.

With the advent of the M16A1, US rifle squads no longer carried an automatic rifle, and had to rely on the platoon's two 7.62mm M60s. These were belt-fed, bipod-mounted guns with quick-change barrels. It would have been better to equip each squad with an M60, which was occasionally done; one M60 per section was the Australian allocation.

Initially each ARVN squad had a .30cal M1918A2 Browning Automatic Rifle, weighing 19.5lb and fed by a 20-round magazine, but these were withdrawn with the issue of M16 rifles. The ARVN's high-priority units received M60s from 1967/68, but most units continued to use the Browning .30cal M1919A6 LMG, which was 9lb heavier than the 23lb M60; this belt-fed gun could be mounted on a tripod, but was more often used on a bipod. Both the M60 and M1919A6 were issued on a scale of only two guns at company level, and after the issue of the M16 rifle platoons and squads had no organic LMGs.

Grenade-launchers

One of the signature weapons of the Vietnam War was the 40mm M79 grenade-launcher – the "blooper" or "thumper." Adopted in 1960, it had its combat debut in Vietnam, where it saw extremely widespread use. This compact little weapon was single-shot and breech-loading. It could throw a high-explosive round at area targets up to 350m away, and at small point targets at 150-plus yards. Since visual ranges were so short in the forests, and there were few clear areas available to set up mortars, the M79 filled the "mortar gap" to some degree. It significantly increased the platoon's firepower, and was generally thought more accurate than rifle-launched grenades (though see the Australian assessment, below). The US Army issued two per squad, and the Marines, Australians, and ARVN one per squad.

Hand grenades were also widely used, owing to the close ranges at which many engagements were fought, and were useful for knocking out bunkers and other fighting positions. Grenades were also useful for small elements, such as reconnaissance patrols, enabling them to break contact with larger enemy forces. In the dense vegetation where visibility was so poor it was common practice to toss as many grenades as rapidly as possible to drive the enemy from his hasty firing positions. This might be done immediately an engagement broke out, to persuade the enemy to break contact and as part of the effort to gain fire superiority. If the enemy were initially outside grenade range, the infantry would attempt to maneuver in closer, and then launch a grenade barrage before closing in for the assault. In the dense vegetation it was difficult to detect incoming grenades being thrown, and to spot where they landed so they could be thrown back or evaded.

Australian assessment of infantry weapons

A contemporary assessment of weapons used in Vietnam provides some insight. The source is *Infantry Battalion – Lessons learned from Vietnam*, published by the Australian Army's Directorate of Infantry Papers in 1973:

"*M16 5.56mm.* A versatile weapon, without the stopping power of the SLR [7.62mm L1A1], and one which requires careful maintenance to avoid stoppages.
(1) Needed for scouts and in ambushes because of its automatic capability.
(2) It has reasonable incapacitating effect up to 100m, but lacks penetrating power in undergrowth.
(3) Easier to handle than the SLR but, because of the large foresight bracket, still catches on undergrowth in very close country.
(4) Needs camouflage painting or taping to stop shine from the fiberglass components.
(5) The lower receiver assembly must be kept well lubricated, but soldiers must not be allowed to strip or tamper with this mechanism.

C CONTACT DRILLS

"Contact/battle/immediate action drills" were originated before World War II by the German Army, and later perfected by British Commonwealth forces; the US was rather late in adopting the concept. These drills provided guidelines for basic reactions to enemy contact; they were standardized, but were not meant to be rigid. Many units developed their own procedures based upon experience, preference, or local terrain, and reactions had to take many factors into consideration – direction of attack, size and disposition of the force, terrain, visibility, volume of fire, and other intangibles. To react effectively required experienced and "savvy" leaders and troops.

C1: A US squad reacts to fire from a bunker, which it assaults. (The same maneuver would be used when running into an enemy patrol or other small element.) The two fire teams might advance alternately, "leap-frogging" forward with one giving covering fire while the other advanced. Alternatively, one team might give sustained covering fire while the other advanced in a series of short rushes. In this case the squad has a machine gun attached. *Personnel key:* **1** = squad leader, **2** = fire-team leader, **3** = grenadier, **4** = riflemen, **5** = MG.
It was seldom that a single NVA/VC bunker was encountered; they were a feature of fortified base camps or defended villages or hills, and each was usually covered by others or by camouflaged foxholes. Attacking a group of them required coordinated action by a whole platoon; typically, one squad would attack a more exposed bunker while the other squads placed suppressive fire on the others. Once the first bunker was neutralized, the next adjacent bunker was vulnerable to attack from a flank, and the enemy position could be "rolled up" by attacking each subsequent bunker in turn.

C2: A US rifle platoon moving in column formation locates an enemy base camp, and it opens fire. The goal is to attack as quickly as possible, and fix the enemy before they can withdraw. Once engaged, the platoon attempts to maneuver two squads to a flank and launch an attack, while one squad and one or two machine guns provide suppressive fire. If the base camp were detected without alerting the enemy, then the platoon might position one or two squads behind it as a blocking force. The remainder of the platoon could then execute a feint attack, to force the enemy to withdraw into the blocking force.

C3a & b: The Australian Task Force made extensive use of battle drills. This example demonstrates a rifle section's reaction when the lead portion of a patrol is ambushed from the right. The section is moving in staggered formation when the scouts and section commander are pinned in a "kill zone." Those outside the kill zone rush to their right, and concentrate to attack the enemy's flank, while the MG group take cover and support the assault by fire. If a subunit was attacked from the front or rear, then if the ambushers were close enough or if their fire was ineffective, those directly engaged might try to assault through the ambushers. If, as was more likely, they were caught in a kill zone and unable to break contact, they would take cover while the rest of the section withdrew out of the danger area and maneuvered to outflank the enemy, or – if the enemy was too strong – to cover by fire the withdrawal of the engaged element. *Personnel key:* **1** = section commander; **2** = 2ic with M79, **3** = scout, **4** = MG group, **5** = riflemen.

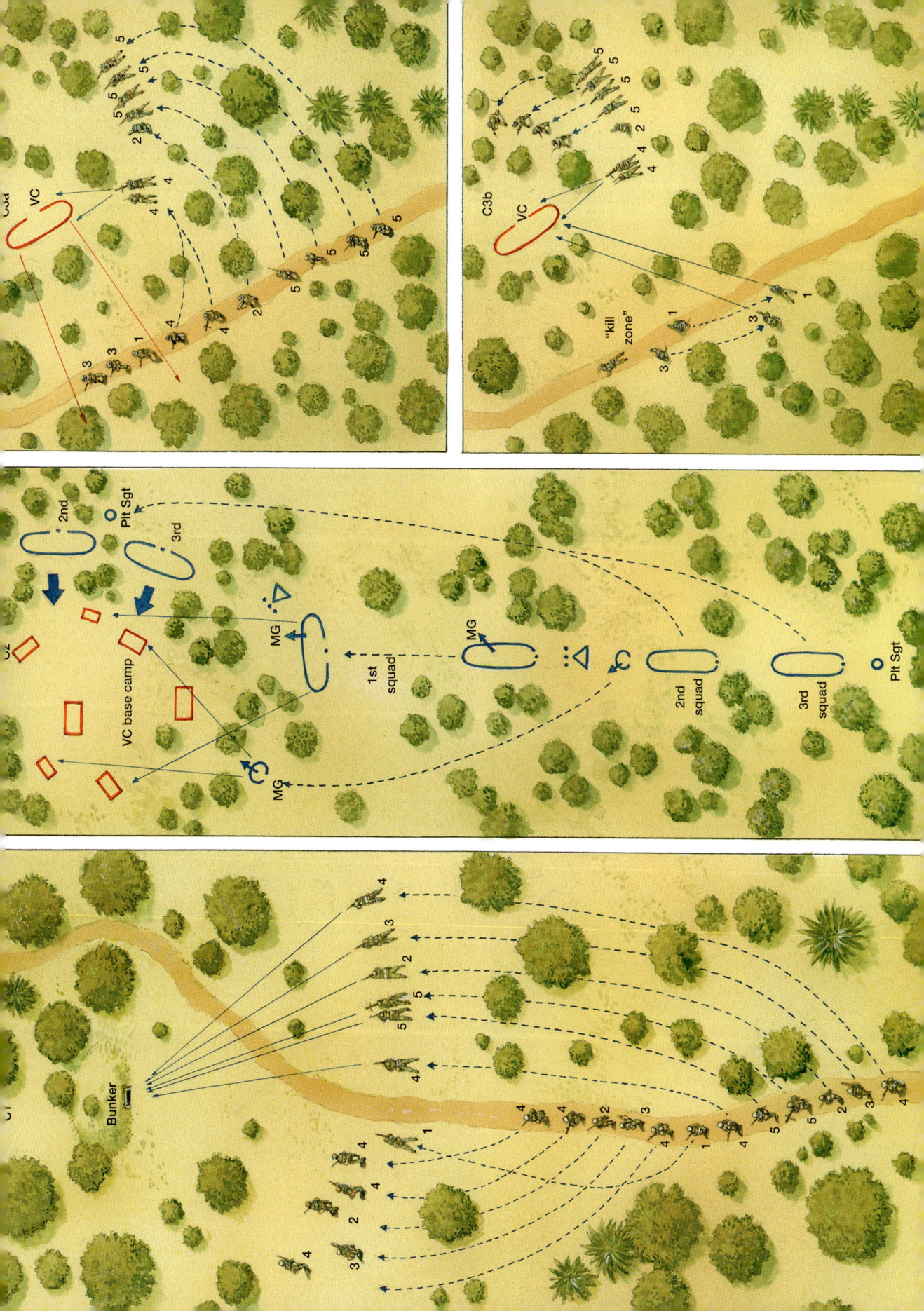

Hand grenades were valuable weapons in jungle fighting, and the infantryman typically carried two to four "frag" grenades. However, in thickly wooded country throwing a grenade required caution: it might be deflected by heavy vegetation, and if it hit a tree it could easily bounce back on the thrower or nearby friendly troops.

(6) Much more effective than the F1 submachine gun.
(7) Present scaling (265) for a battalion is adequate.

SMG 9mm F1. A light, reliable, and easily handled weapon which should be most useful because of its automatic capability. In practice it lacks incapacitating power, and does not now appear to deserve a place in an infantry battalion equipment table. A small pool has been suggested for use in village searches and inner cordons.

GPMG [General Purpose Machine Gun] M60. A reliable (when well maintained) machine gun, which has proved its worth in action.
(1) It is heavy and cumbersome to handle, too much so for general patrol and section work.
(2) There is a tendency to regard the M60 as a personal rather than a crew weapon in which every soldier must be thoroughly trained, particularly in advanced handling by day and night.
(3) Particular components have in the past broken too easily. These have largely been, or are being rectified.

(4) The biggest disadvantage is the carriage of belt ammunition. It is awkward, the links splay easily, and it readily collects dirt and mud. Various methods have been tried for carrying the belts, from Claymore bags, pouches utility, to specially manufactured waterproof covers.

(5) The biggest advantage is its dependable sustained fire. The new scaling of 28 per battalion in a pool is considered adequate for the sustained fire role.

90mm RCL [M67 Recoilless Rifle]. Is mainly used in defensive locations or ambushes close to the base (flechette round thought valuable), as too heavy to patrol with.

Grenades. Rifle grenades performed better than the M79 grenade-launcher or M72 LAW (although it looks like a training deficiency caused problems early on). [US] M26 hand grenades projected from the rifle [with an issue add-on tailboom and fin assembly] are extremely accurate and successful against bunker systems. Projected grenades are far superior to the M79 and M72 in secondary jungle, and must be carried in quantity."

MOBILITY

Airmobility

Among Free World Forces there were several means of delivery onto the battlefield, but the predominant means was airmobile assault, by helicopter.[3] Airmobility gave ground forces unprecedented mobility and support, to seize terrain, envelop enemy dispositions, deprive the enemy of required resources, divert his attention, and destroy his forces. The airmobile assault supported all types of offensive operations: movement to contact, reconnaissance-in-force, raids, limited-objective attacks, coordinated attacks, exploitation, and pursuit. The assault force could get into an area quickly, assault deeply into enemy territory, and bypass intervening enemy forces and rough terrain. Airmobility allowed the frontal attack to be avoided, and provided the ability to rapidly reinforce successful attacks and resupply engaged forces. Helicopters also provided valuable fire support, command and control, reconnaissance, surveillance, and medical evacuation.

The airmobile assault was essentially a movement-to-contact. The ground force was delivered into enemy territory by helicopters, and then moved on foot to engage him. The enemy was usually encountered in a meeting engagement. The force seizing the initiative in a meeting engagement has the advantage; airmobility enhanced the capacity of the Free World force to achieve this, because of its ability to move rapidly, bypassing rough terrain, reinforcing or repositioning units, and resupplying them. Blocking forces could be inserted to engage a withdrawing enemy (pursuit). A reserve was essential, for reinforcement, exploiting success, insertion as a blocking force, or attacking from another direction. Reserve and reaction forces were usually kept on "strip-alert," with helicopters on standby for immediate commitment.

Airmobility kept the enemy off balance; in so-called "Jitterbug" operations, companies and even platoons could be leap-frogged around the

This member of a New Zealand SAS patrol carries a 7.62mm L1A1 self-loading rifle (SLR), with minor examples of the modifications typical of ANZAC special forces: removal of the carrying handle, sling swivels and muzzle-flash suppressor. Hung from his web gear are American M67 "baseball," M18 smoke, and M34 white phosphorus grenades. (Photo NZ Army PR)

3. See Elite 154: *Vietnam Airmobile Warfare Tactics*

UH-1 Huey "slicks" inbound to a landing zone. Owing to the weight of machine guns, ammunition, troop combat loads, and the heat and humidity (air density), in Vietnam Hueys could not carry their advertized weight. Usually only five or six infantrymen could be transported along with the four-man crew.

Armored troop carriers (ATCs) of the Mobile Riverine Force cruising on a waterway in the Mekong Delta. Each well-armed ATC carried a rifle platoon from the 9th Infantry Division.

area of operations (AO) by helicopter to make contact with an elusive enemy. It enabled a rapid response, and an ability to move and insert forces that made it almost impossible for the NVA/VC to fully press home attacks on Free World installations. When the cloak of darkness was raised at dawn they simply ran out of time to overrun their objective before the helicopters appeared. Helicopters were, of course, hampered by bad weather, slowed by the range they had to travel from bases, and limited by the lack of suitable landing zones in some areas.

Water transport

This was a lesser-used means of providing mobility, but riverine operations were extensively conducted by the US 9th Infantry Division and the ARVN in the wetlands of the Mekong Delta. Specially modified riverine assault craft and patrol boats were used on the countless rivers, creeks, and canals of this region.[4] Such operations had the disadvantage of slow movement along predictable routes that were easily kept under surveillance by the enemy, who could execute ambushes from thick cover at short ranges. Nonetheless, such operations could deliver large numbers of troops, who need not be heavily burdened because of the nearby support of the assault craft. Airmobile operations also inserted troops in support of waterborne units.

4. See New Vanguard 128: *Vietnam Riverine Craft 1962–75*, which also discusses tactics.

Mechanized tactics

At one time or another the US had eight mechanized battalions in Vietnam. Besides offensive operations on suitable terrain, they conducted line-of-communications security missions and convoy escort, and escorted self-propelled and towed artillery between firebases. In Vietnam there was more viable operational terrain for them (and for the 10 battalion-sized armored cavalry squadrons, and three tank battalions) than many planners had envisioned. The ARVN and the Australian Task Force also made good use of armored cavalry and tank units. All the mechanized units were equipped with M113A1 armored personnel carriers and modified M113 armored cavalry assault vehicles (APCs and ACAVs). The US Marine Corps employed two tank and two amphibian tractor battalions; while not APCs, the large, cumbersome "amtracs" were used to haul troops and conduct mounted patrols, but were limited to moderate and mostly level terrain.

An M113A1 ACAV being prepared for an operation. The infantry ride on top – seemingly in an exposed position, but far safer from mines and RPGs than they would be inside the vehicle. Mechanized units could carry heavier weapons – note the 90mm M67 recoilless rifle visible to the left of the .50cal MG shield. Ammunition crates are being loaded behind the extended bow plane, normally used when "swimming" the vehicle.

Besides operations on lines of communications, mechanized units made sweeps across moderate terrain, relying on their firepower and armor protection to overcome resistance. One goal was to flush out the enemy and push them into infantry blocking forces waiting in ambush. In moderately wooded and heavy brush areas a dozer-tank would lead a (usually) mixed unit of tanks and mechanized infantry, plowing a winding path following terrain contours; this was called a "tank-bust." The NVA/VC would mine these, in hopes of catching AFVs traveling on old tank-busts, but this was usually avoided, and new paths would be plowed on subsequent operations. Over time, dozens of tank-busts snaked through some areas, but they were quickly reclaimed by the jungle. Because of fallen trees, tangled limbs, stumps, and roots, all intermingled with brush and vines, they were little used by infantry on either side; however, they did provide narrow exposed lanes, where enemy might be detected by scout helicopters while crossing.

Mechanized forces might be used in imaginative ways. One technique was for a mechanized unit to halt for a break or overnight while sweeping through

The ARVN relied heavily on 2½-ton cargo trucks for tactical mobility. They did not possess the same degree of helicopter support as the US forces, but they did conduct frequent airmobile operations using Vietnamese Air Force and US helicopters.

an area, and to leave stay-behind reconnaissance patrols or ambush parties when they departed. In one instance, the author's company of Cambodian "Strikers" were to be inserted in a distant area, but the scheduled helicopters were canceled. A mechanized company at a nearby 1st Infantry Division firebase offered to run the company to its AO. Each M113A1 was manned only by the driver and gunner/commander; the Strike Force company were loaded atop the tracks, and barreled down a road to their AO in 30 minutes – a trip that would have taken a day on foot.

Mechanized units could create an "instantaneous firebase" when they halted for the night. Bristling with guns, the APCs and tanks positioned themselves at close intervals around the perimeter; self-propelled mortars were registered, anti-RPG screens of chain-link fencing were erected in front of the "tracks," and forward listening posts were established. Such a perimeter was deadly to attack.

MOVEMENT ON FOOT

While 2½-ton cargo trucks were occasionally used to transport troops on secure roads, and the ARVN relied heavily on them, the principal means of movement by all combatants was their own two feet – whether in the jungles, swamps, hills, or plains.

The standard military rate of march was 4mph, with a 10-minute break every hour, but in Vietnam nothing was "standard." There were areas in which good time could be made, and instances in which it was possible to use roads and trails. Roads used by convoys and commercial traffic during the day were for all practical purposes abandoned to the enemy at nightfall. They were not reopened until infantry-escorted engineers had swept the road and shoulders visually and with mine detectors. These road-clearing parties worked in both directions from firebases securing the route, meeting up midway. Before returning to base they radioed back, and waiting convoys and buses were allowed to proceed. However, the normal rule was to stay off of trails and roads; they might be ambushed, mined, booby-trapped, or at least under surveillance. Sometimes the VC booby-trapped the sides of trails, hoping to catch troops moving parallel to the route.

While maps might be accurate, they did not give much of an idea as to what the ground was actually like. The density of brush and high grass was not depicted, nor was there any indication of the surface – the ground might be smooth, cut by countless gullies, or covered by loose rock. It might be marshy or bone-dry at different times of the year, and there was always the chance of encountering the unexpected. On one occasion the author's company discovered a ridge top (repeat, *top*) completely inundated by a swamp. On another occasion, when hovering just feet above an LZ covered with sword grass being flattened by the downdraft from the rotors, the pilots, crew, and author all agreed that it was dry. We dropped out of the choppers a few feet above the grass – and plunged into 4ft of water.

Men of a command group pass through a forested area largely devoid of underbrush. Note the box-like assembly behind the RTO's right shoulder; this is a loudspeaker for the AN/PRC-25 radio, allowing it to be heard without having one's ear glued to the handset. Noise discipline was not a priority in units using these.

A platoon crossing a flooded rice paddy in a line formation; trudging across an entire valley of flooded paddies was a long and tiring process. Notice the contrasts in the terrain – rice paddies, a forested area, and jungle-covered hills, all in close proximity.

Most movement was cross-country, and was a slow, cautious process. There was no average rate of march, since the terrain and vegetation varied so greatly, even within a small area. A unit might find itself moving easily across level, forested ground with little underbrush; then virtually crawling to get through a broad band of bamboo thicket; then pushing through dense brush, only to emerge into a series of rice paddies that had to be crossed while totally exposed; then wading through a bordering area of marsh, and into head-high elephant grass flooded ankle-deep in water; and finally clambering up a ridge, densely covered with brush and trees and crisscrossed by gullies – and all within an hour or two. In many areas open rice paddies were too extensive to be bypassed, and had to be crossed. They might be rock-hard and dry, muddy, or flooded. They were divided up into individual paddies by low, narrow dikes; if the fields were flooded these served as footpaths, but troops using these narrow causeways were exposed to fire and booby traps.

The preferred method of crossing a flooded rice paddy, boots dry. A security element would be sent across first to check the far side, then the rest of the unit would file across the dikes.

A particularly troublesome type of obstacle were "Arc Light" tracks – long swathes of bomb craters, sometimes a couple of miles long by a few hundred yards wide – which marked the passing of a "cell" of three B-52 bombers, dropping scores of heavy bombs on prescribed paths. The massive blasts uprooted and shattered trees, leaving stumps, roots, trunks, and torn limbs tangled together; in the tropical climate brush, saplings, and vines grew up rapidly, concealing the deep craters and the tangled chaos of smashed timber. Crossing these corridors of destruction was extremely slow and difficult, and injuries might be expected.

The phrase "busting brush" aptly describes the experience of passing through particularly dense vegetation. It was difficult for heavily burdened troops to move through such vegetation quietly, and the larger the body of troops the more of a challenge it was. Machetes were seldom used to hack paths through brush; apart from the noise, it was more physically wearing than just pushing through the undergrowth. Only the smallest, most highly trained, and very slow-moving patrols could pass without leaving much of a telltale trail behind them. A rifle platoon would leave a very distinct trail, and a company even more so. It was thus very easy for an enemy patrol to track a unit if they discovered the signs of its passing soon enough. It was impossible to cover a unit's tracks, as the thickly layered fallen leaves and humus were easily disturbed. The same applied to bamboo leaves, the path made through elephant grass, and the stirred-up mud trail left across marshes and wet rice paddies. (Dragging a leafy tree limb in hopes of disguising a trail only disturbed the ground-cover even more.)

Movement formations

In conventional warfare, small units were taught a variety of geometric movement formations: line, column, wedge, inverted wedge ("V"), and echelon (slanting line). In Vietnam there was, of course, some terrain on which conventional subunit formations were viable and useful, but the terrain and tactical situation often dictated different solutions (see Plates A & B). Most often, subunits moved in single-file columns, occasionally with two or three

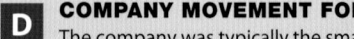

COMPANY MOVEMENT FORMATIONS
The company was typically the smallest unit to operate semi-independently; the platoon might operate for brief periods at short distances from the company, but seldom without support. Companies might operate in standard formations: the column **(D1)**, line **(D2)**, "V" **(D3)**, inverted "V" wedge **(D4)**, or echeloned **(D5)**. However, the "long green line" column formation was by far the most common. Companies also used two-column **(D6)** and three-column **(D7)** formations in areas where the underbrush was lighter; the former required that some elements be split between the two columns. In the three-column formation – actually, a line, with the three platoons in column – it was easier to maintain control than when the middle platoon was forward or to the rear, as in a wedge or "V" company formation. (Small flanking elements might be employed, but are not shown here.) Another formation, used in moderate vegetation, was the "box" **(D8)**, with one platoon on line forward and the other two in column. If attacked from the front or flank by a superior force it could close up into a triangular formation **(D9)**; alternatively, either flank platoon could swing up into the line, or maneuver to outflank the enemy. Formations were usually kept simple, to ease command and control and to better keep track of subunits when contacts occurred. An 81mm mortar squad is shown in all these images; there might be two, but probably no mortars were carried. A US Marine company might have one to three 60mm mortars.

The rifle company HQ was assigned 10–13 men depending on the type of company, but most of them remained with the company rear element. In the field the company command group **(D10)** typically consisted of the CO **(1)**, the XO or 1st sergeant **(2)**, an artillery FO **(3)**, and about three radio operators **(4)**. Usually either the XO or the 1st sergeant remained with the company rear element. Many companies had a "field 1st sergeant," a senior NCO who accompanied the company while the 1st sergeant remained in the rear. The XO and/or 1st sergeant would in fact usually be elsewhere in the formation, or roving to check on subunits.

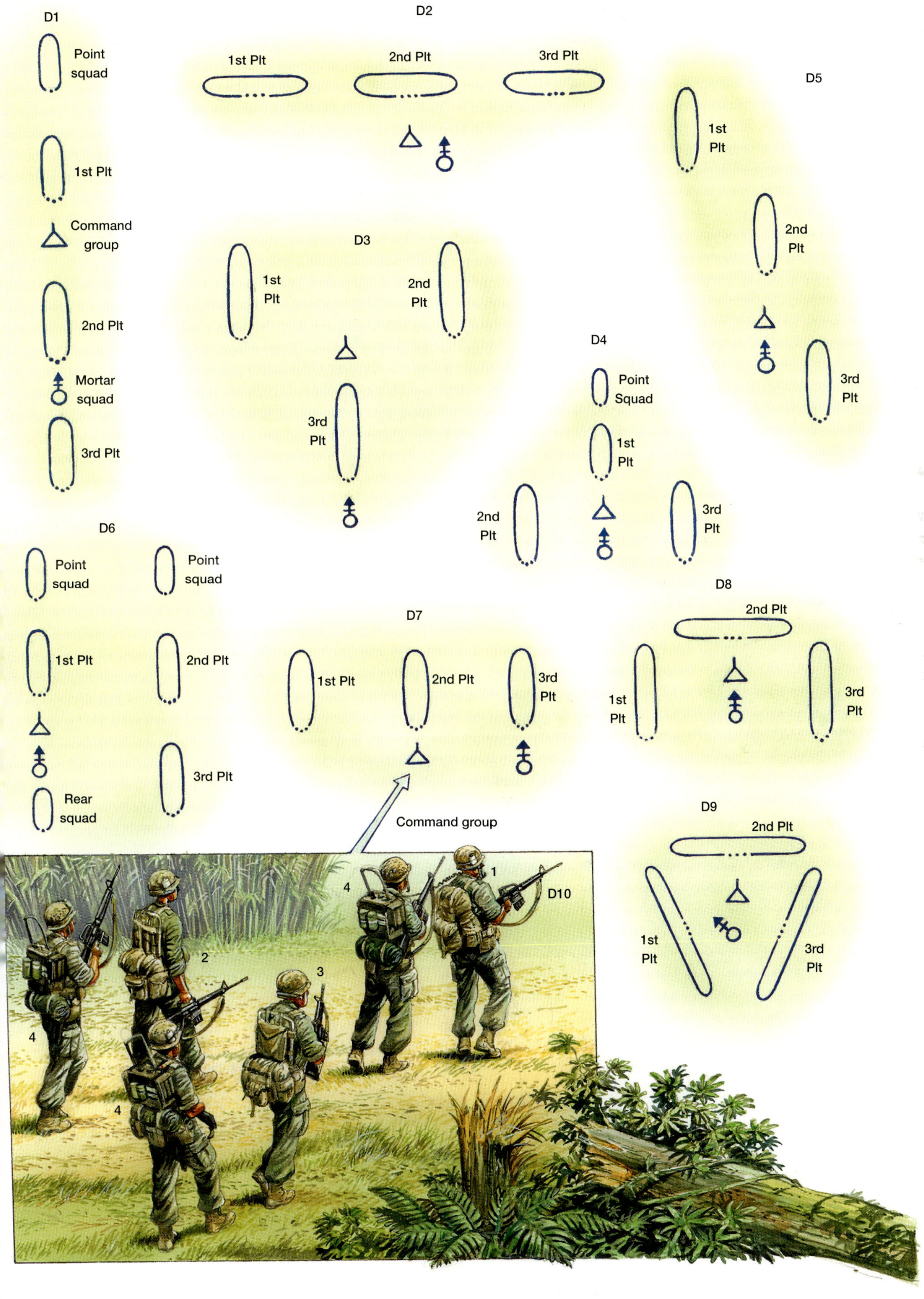
D1
Point squad
1st Plt
Command group
2nd Plt
Mortar squad
3rd Plt
D2
1st Plt
2nd Plt
3rd Plt
D3
1st Plt
2nd Plt
3rd Plt
D4
Point Squad
1st Plt
2nd Plt
3rd Plt
D5
1st Plt
2nd Plt
3rd Plt
D6
Point squad
Point squad
1st Plt
2nd Plt
3rd Plt
Rear squad
D7
1st Plt
2nd Plt
3rd Plt
Command group
D8
2nd Plt
1st Plt
3rd Plt
D9
2nd Plt
1st Plt
3rd Plt
D10
1
2
3
4
4
4

Troops could hop easily across meandering streams in the dry seasons, but in the June-to-October monsoon rains these flooded, creating a formidable obstacle for infantry. Once the boots were wet they would remain so all day, and this drastically increased the blister rate. The foreground man (right photo) carries an M79 grenade-launcher and wears a grenadier's ammunition vest, with pockets for 18 rounds of 40mm HE and four pyrotechnic rounds.

parallel columns moving in close proximity. Ideally, they would move in the more dispersed formations, but the reality was that these were slow-moving and noisy (since each man had to break his own path). They were also difficult to control in the limited visibility imposed by thick vegetation, and dispersal made "friendly fire" incidents more frequent.

The typical deployment of a Free World battalion was for its companies to operate semi-independently, but within a mile or two of one another. They would move on specific routes or to designated objectives. Some might attempt to push the enemy toward blocking forces, which might ambush likely withdrawal routes. When working toward specific objectives such as villages, suspected enemy positions or base camps, or to intercept moving enemy forces, companies would operate in concert under battalion control.

Companies moved in formations as dispersed as the terrain permitted (see Plate D). In dense vegetation this might be a single file – the "long green line," as the Americans called it. In lighter vegetation a company moved in two parallel columns within sight of one other. The two columns might be "balanced," i.e. of roughly equal composition accomplished by splitting some elements, but more commonly one column would consist of one platoon and the other of two. The trailing second platoon would be prepared to maneuver to either flank when the head of either of the two columns made contact. In rare instances a company might move in three platoon columns, but this was difficult to control.

If flank security was used at all, it too remained in sight; men sent out for flank security had to break their own trail, which made more noise, slowed them down, and exposed them to the risks of being mistaken for the enemy or becoming separated. Rear security was essential, however, and ambushes were left on the back-trail to hit any following enemy. Stream crossings were especially good places to leave an ambush. Another method used to counter a following enemy was to send an ambush patrol looping out to circle back and ambush the unit's back-trail from the flank. Another counter-tracking technique was for a unit to change direction every few hundred yards, to keep the following enemy guessing as to its route or ultimate destination. Enemy tracking teams sometimes trailed units by following a parallel course, to lessen the chance of being detected by their quarry, but it was easy for them to lose contact with a unit this way. When a Free World unit halted for rest breaks a perimeter would be formed; security outposts would be established a short distance away, and ambushes might be set up on the back-trail and elsewhere.

Stream crossings were dangerous in their own right. A unit crossing a stream inevitably slowed down as the troops negotiated the obstacle, and filled their canteens. The head of the column had to slow their pace to give the rest of the unit time to catch up. The prudent commander would establish security to the flanks and rear when crossing a stream or a similar obstacle such as a ravine.

The dispersal of individual soldiers was naturally desirable, so that a single automatic-weapon burst, grenade, or mortar round would not take out several men, but the intervals between individuals had to vary depending on visibility. The denser the vegetation, the smaller the interval, as it was essential for individuals to maintain visual contact; if they lost sight of one another they might become separated from the unit, or the formation would be disrupted. In very dense vegetation the interval had to be close, and at night individuals had to be almost touching. Even on a starry moonlit night, it was so dark in the jungle that men had to grip the web gear or pack of the man in front so as not to lose contact. Quiet movement at night, except for small teams, was almost impossible, owing to stumbling and breaking vegetation. The NVA/VC habitually used flashlights during night movement, both to find their way and for fear of snakes. When using flashlights Free World troops often fitted red filters; eliminating most of the glare, these made it difficult to detect the light from a distance, and protected the men's night vision.

There were more open areas, in the Central Highlands and elsewhere, where large clearings were too broad to skirt around, or rice paddies could not always be bypassed. On encountering these the platoons would deploy on line or in wedge formations (inverted "V"), to make their way across quickly. Of course, in such cases it was highly likely that VC lookouts or VC-sympathizing civilians would report the passage of Free World troops. Except in the most remote, unpopulated regions, it was likely that the NVA/VC in the area knew

In thick, slick mud it could be a three-man job to get one heavily loaded man up a stream bank. It might take an hour for a company more than 100 strong to cross such an obstacle.

where Free World units were located, and tracked their movements. In populated rural areas observation by civilians could not be avoided. There were villages, farmers in their fields and paddies, woodcutters, fishermen, hunters, children tending animals, roadside vendors, and travelers on roads and trails, and any of these might report the presence, numbers, and movement direction of Free World troops. The VC unit responsible for the area would receive reports from runners; they would plot the unit's movements, and sometimes they might be able to determine its objective as the different companies converged on it. They also deployed small patrols throughout their areas, especially in underpopulated regions.

Engagements

If engaged, the reactions of a unit or patrol would depend on its strength, the enemy's strength, the mission, and the tactical advantage held by one side or the other. The pointman typically opened fire on full-automatic, and fell back. The backup men did the same, and threw grenades; if facing a superior enemy force they might also pop smoke grenades to cover the withdrawal. A small element engaged by a superior enemy force might be ordered to break contact and withdraw; otherwise, the remainder of the unit/patrol would deploy left and right on line, to place the maximum amount of firepower on the enemy. Grenade-launchers and machine guns would be moved into position as rapidly as possible, to help gain fire superiority. Precautions had to be taken to ensure the enemy was not attempting to outflank the unit, and security had to be maintained to the rear – if the enemy force was large enough, such an attempt would soon be made.

If the friendly force was large enough, it too would begin outflanking maneuvers (see Plate C). The NVA/VC would often "thin" their center sector

---

E — PATROLLING TECHNIQUES

Effective patrols required a detailed search of a designated area to locate any enemy activity. A map reconnaissance of the area would identify points of interest, but the enemy was very adept at selecting positions in unlikely terrain. Most patrols were of platoon size – smaller patrols might not survive an engagement.

E1: Major-General Raymond Davis, commanding 3d Marine Division, explained: "A company will be put into an area 2km or 3km on a side [1.2–1.85 miles]. They'll cut an LZ for resupply and medevac, and they'll work day [patrolling] and night [ambush] activities until they've thoroughly searched out this area. By thoroughly searching out, I mean on every trail, every small knob, every draw, every finger [of hillside] – total search-out of the area. They would then be lifted to another place." In such circumstances the company would move as an entity, but platoons would be dispatched on "cloverleaf" searches of areas of interest.

E2: "Jitterbug" operations saw a battalion deployed with one company defending the firebase, another on "strip alert" as an airmobile reaction force, and two companies committed to platoon-size area reconnaissance missions. A 12km × 12km area (7.5 × 7.5 miles) might be divided up into 16 grid boxes of 3km × 3km (1.85 × 1.85 miles), and the six available platoons of the two companies would be inserted in an irregular pattern, to thoroughly search their assigned box. This example shows a smaller area of 6km × 6km (3.7 × 3.7 miles), divided into nine boxes of 2km × 2km (1.2 × 1.2 miles), to be reconnoitered by a single company augmented by the battalion recon platoon. Platoons would spend a day or two searching, and then move by foot or helicopter into another "box," until all had been searched. Some boxes would be searched a second time, in case the enemy had shifted into an already-searched area. If a platoon made contact, other nearby platoons would move to support them, and the reaction company would be inserted to reinforce or to establish a blocking position.

E3: "Bushmaster" operations saw the insertion of platoons into sparsely vegetated areas in the last two hours of daylight. A central CP was established, and the platoons occupied areas within 750 yards of one another, for mutual support in case of contact. After dark, the platoons occupied ambush positions to interdict enemy movement, especially if signs of activity were discovered. Here, a platoon HQ (triangle) and three squad ambush positions are indicated. An offshoot of the "bushmaster" was the "checkerboard." The next morning, the platoons broke down into squads to occupy a grid-square pattern. The squads moved continuously from square to square, to locate small enemy elements. This was not wise in an area where the enemy was present in strength. Since these were only two-day operations, the troops carried limited ammunition and rations to allow them to move easily.

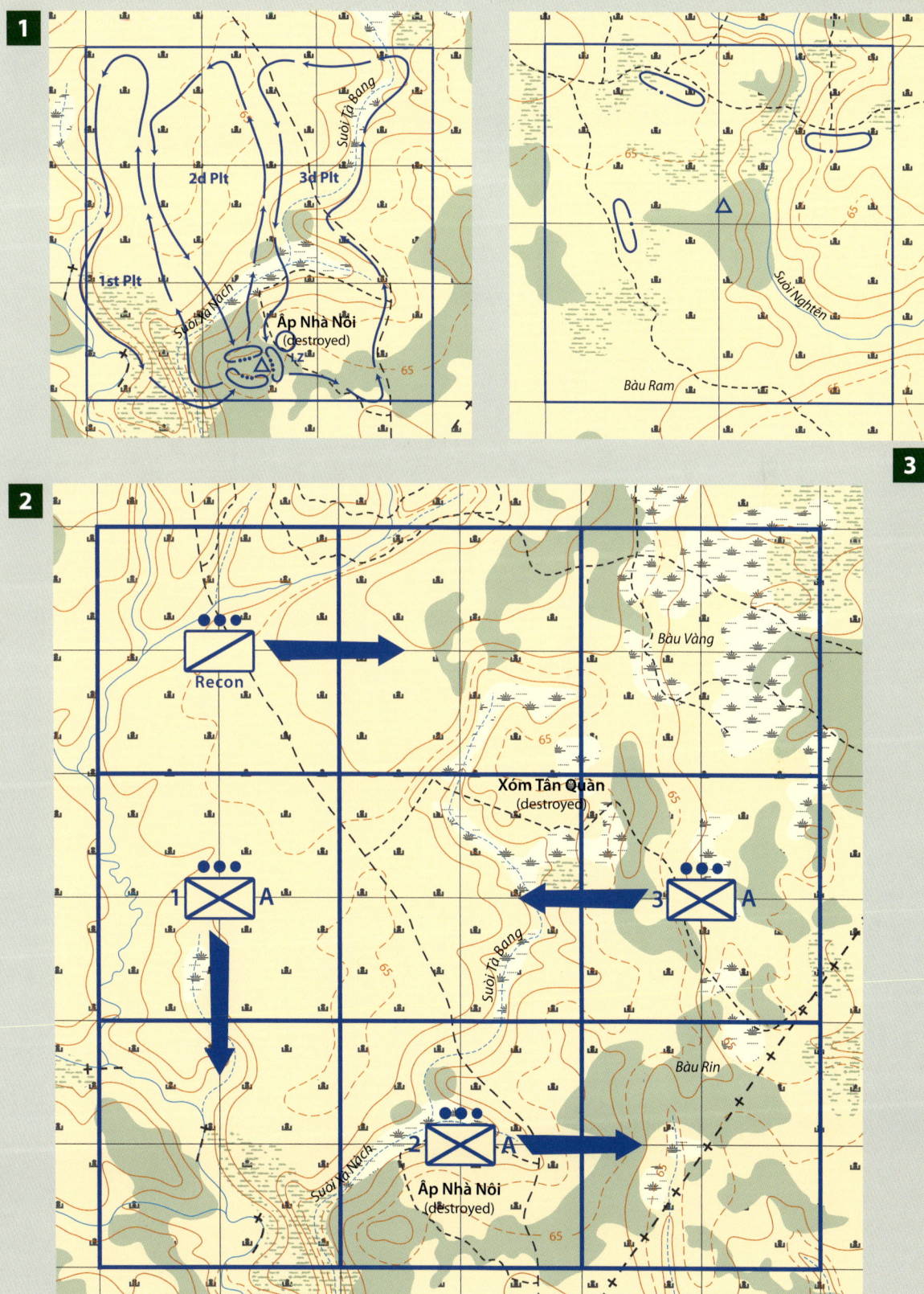

Contact! Infantrymen fire blindly into tall grass and trees to flush out any enemy as they advance. The enemy were in fact seldom seen, even at close ranges, and when they were seen it was only in fleeting glimpses lasting mere seconds.

when an engagement had been initiated, and begin sending elements to their flanks to engage outflanking Free World elements. However, the enemy would leave sufficient forces in the center to keep the Free World force from disengaging or attacking through the thinned front. Commanders were expected to radio a contact report immediately to their higher headquarters, reporting their own and the enemy's location, who initiated contact, and casualties to that point. Depending on the situation, artillery fire might be requested, and this would arrive within minutes. The NVA/VC expected this, and attempted to "hug" the Free World positions to prevent the artillery from falling on them; this tactic also hampered any helicopter gunships and CAS that might arrive on the scene.

Often the battalion commander would arrive in a command-and-control (C&C) chopper and orbit overhead. This practice has often been condemned, and justly so in some instances. There was a very real danger of the airborne commander losing touch with the realities on the ground: from above, distances seemed to shrink, and dense vegetation and rough ground hidden beneath the forest canopy could not be appreciated. The airborne commander might overestimate the response capabilities of exhausted, stressed troops in contact. On the other hand, being airborne gave the commander a broad view of the battlefield, and he might see variances in the terrain unseen by a ground commander with only restricted visibility. The airborne CO could relieve the already overburdened ground commander of dealing with fire control, and could coordinate additional assets. Most battalion commanders had previously commanded companies, and did appreciate the realities on the ground.

Once an enemy force was engaged with fire and maneuver in an effort to fix it, every effort was made to destroy it. Fire support was coordinated; reaction forces might be inserted by helicopter, and other units moved on the ground to reinforce, attack from another direction, block the enemy's withdrawal, and pursue if necessary. Often other enemy units were located in the area during the engagement, and the action escalated.

The "RON"

The "remain overnight" (RON) position was typically of company or battalion size (see Plate H). Even when companies were operating dispersed they might assemble at a common position for the night, especially when there was a threat of a heavy enemy attack. Ideally, a unit would halt for supper before last light, and would move a short distance to the RON under limited visibility, making it difficult to determine their deployment and exact position. Sometimes this was not possible because of the density of vegetation, when possible fields of fire had to be cleared – a noisy affair.

Two-man fighting positions were dug around the perimeter, where one man remained on guard and the other slept ("50-percent alert"). Often a sleeping position – a shallow, prone foxhole – was dug to the rear of the fighting position where the man on guard was stationed. Some units went so far as to use chainsaws to cut down trees and build small fighting bunkers, having the chainsaws, picks, and shovels helicoptered in. Claymores (command-detonated directional antipersonnel mines) and trip flares had to be emplaced, artillery concentrations were plotted around the RON in case of need, and machine guns were sited to cover as much of the perimeter as possible.

Two- or three-man listening posts (LPs) were sent out a short distance to detect the sounds of enemy movement, the number depending on the terrain and vegetation. Obvious avenues of approach were relatively unimportant, since the enemy would attempt to infiltrate over the most unlikely and difficult ground. The LPs needed to be in radio or telephone contact with the command post (CP), otherwise the only ways to alert the parent unit were either to run back or to open fire – either of which could be fatal. Some units did not deploy LPs, since these would inevitably be exposed and cut off if the enemy attacked.

Noise and light discipline were critical, but admittedly many conventional units were lax in this regard. It was not unknown for units with low morale – US, ARVN, but also some NVA/VC – to make noise intentionally in order to warn the enemy away. The construction of fighting positions and clearing of fields of fire were extremely noisy, and during this work such units made no attempt to maintain noise discipline. The enemy generally avoided such units,

An M60 machine gunner sweeps fire across an area covered with sword grass. Even low grass like this was extremely slow and tiring to move through – and it could grow head-high or even taller, cutting visibility to zero and trapping the stifling heat.

but might take advantage of their poor field skills to attack or harass them at will. It was not only the troops who were poorly disciplined and lacked tactical proficiency; many conventionally minded officers ignored the basic precepts of guerrilla warfare. On the other hand, there were units that occupied their RON quietly, prepared minimal positions, emplaced Claymores and trip flares without clearing fields of fire, and established ambushes on likely avenues of approach. Such units were almost invariably more successful than those that were less disciplined.

Ideally the RON's shape would be triangular, with a company/platoon on each side of a battalion/company position. However, units took advantage of terrain, and RONs conformed to available cover and concealment such as clumps of trees or other dense vegetation, gullies, dikes, streambeds, canals, rivers, or roads. Perimeters might also be roughly circular, oval, or irregular in shape. Battalion and company command posts, the aid station, and the supply point would be established.

If temporary bases were established in the AO during the course of an operation, many units followed the rule of avoiding remaining in one location for more than three nights. The NVA/VC would avoid the location on the first night. On the second, the unit's continuing presence alerted them to the fact that it might plan to remain there. On the third night they would conduct a reconnaissance, and then plan an attack. If the unit remained for a fourth night, that was when it would be attacked.

To allow companies to remain in the field for several days and nights, chow was sometimes flown in. Typically they would be resupplied by helicopter every three days – a "minor resup," with ration packs and other essential supplies. If they were out that long, every six days they received a "major resup," with hot chow, replacement clothing, mail, etc. This might be a rest day, if the operational situation permitted.

FIRE SUPPORT

This was the area of greatest imbalance between Free World and NVA/VC forces. For the Free World Forces, the ever-critical support was provided by field artillery from firebases, helicopter gunships, and ground-attack aircraft. For the NVA/VC, it was limited to man-portable rockets, mortars, recoilless weapons, and machine guns (as well as sappers, whose charges were used as a form of "man-delivered artillery"). The challenge for Free World Forces was to place effective fire into large areas – so-called "free fire zones" – because of the wide dispersal of the enemy. The NVA/VC were faced with the opposite problem: to deliver firepower into a small area – Free World bases and other installations.

Artillery
The Free World Forces employed artillery designed for accurate fire in a conventional war, while the NVA/VC had less-accurate rockets and mortars delivering only moderate firepower. On the other hand, it was easy for them to hit bases; they knew where they were, and could pre-position weapons

Artillery support was absolutely essential; Free World conventional units never operated outside artillery range, and there were almost as many US artillery battalions in Vietnam as infantry battalions. Here, a 105mm M102 howitzer crew prepare for a fire mission. The lightweight M102 was used by airborne and airmobile artillery battalions; other units used the heavier 105mm M101A1 howitzer dating from World War II (when it was designated the M2A1).

and ammunition to range them. What was known as the "rocket belt" was an 8,000–12,000-yard band around large installations, from which rockets were launched, and through which Free World patrols and aerial surveillance were conducted night and day. However, it was not enough for the NVA/VC just to hit a base; divisional bases and airbases occupied a great deal of ground, and facilities were dispersed, so a dozen 122mm rockets could be fired into a large base without inflicting any damage whatsoever.

Free World Forces had abundant artillery. Late in the war there were 64 US Army artillery battalions, 10 US Marine, 50 ARVN, eight Korean, four Thai, and one Australian/New Zealand battalion. Most battalions had three batteries each with six 105mm or 155mm howitzers, while batteries of 8in (203mm) and 175mm (7.8in) guns had four pieces each. Ample artillery was available to support units making sporadic contacts scattered over an area of operations. This was accomplished by establishing mutually supporting firebases arranged to provide an umbrella of overlapping fires throughout entire regions. These might be atop hills and ridges, or on flat ground set in clearings suitable for helicopter landing zones. Firebases might be maintained in semi-permanent status, protecting lines of communications and population centers, but most were established for short periods – weeks, or just a few days – in order to expand the area covered by fire to support specific operations. Such bases typically held one or two batteries – one of 105mm and the other 155mm, or a 105mm battery and just two 155mm howitzers – protected by a rifle company. Free World units never operated without artillery support except in rare special cases.

A 155mm M114A1 howitzer in full recoil. The steel tubes in the revetment wall are expended and earth-filled containers for propellant bags.

Heavier and longer-ranged artillery was available in the form of 175mm guns and 8in howitzers. The heavy artillery was usually located at semi-permanent firebases containing an artillery battalion-plus, or at brigade or division bases; these larger bases would also have 155mm and 105mm batteries or even battalions.

The ability to "helio-lift" artillery into remote clearings and quickly establish a firebase provided a great deal of flexibility in the support of infantry operations. Army CH-47 Chinook and Marine CH-53A Sea Stallion helicopters could lift a 105mm. Lifting the 155mm required the Army's CH-54A "Flying Crane" or the Marines' CH-37A Mojave or CH-53A Sea Stallion. Since the infantry were likewise rapidly inserted at different points throughout an area, with the artillery almost as quickly emplaced to support them, the enemy was kept off balance and had to be prepared for a thrust from any direction. This required both enemy units and supply dumps (caches) to remain widely dispersed. While the NVA/VC had the ability to move and concentrate forces rapidly, they could not even approach the speed achievable by airmobility.

Targets were preplanned to support an operation. The Free World infantry unit would know the locations or projected locations of supporting firebases and the calibers of the guns, thus allowing it to plot targets capitalizing on the different weapons' capabilities and positioning. It was preferable to assign targets to batteries that were on a gun-to-target line perpendicular to the infantry's route or deployment line. Firebases were also located in order to place fire on ridge sides by firing down valleys and parallel to the ridge line, rather than attempting to shoot over the ridge and dropping rounds inaccurately on the reverse slope. This is why multiple firebases were established, scattered throughout an area of operations.

Preplanned target reference points (TRP) would be plotted along roads and trails, around clearings and villages, on likely enemy ambush sites, at stream crossings, and in areas where the enemy might assemble. If contact with the enemy was made, the artillery fire would be adjusted from the TRP onto the enemy. At night, final defensive fires or defensive concentrations would be plotted to surround a RON position with a wall of steel. Fires would also be plotted on possible enemy assembly, attack, and supporting weapons positions, as well as his expected withdrawal routes.

Air support

Almost as responsive as artillery was air support. Close air support (CAS) in the form of fighter-bombers could be on-station within an hour, and often less

The Bell AH-1G Hueycobra gunship was introduced in Vietnam in 1967. This Cobra mounts a six-barrel 7.62mm Minigun and a 40mm automatic grenade-launcher in the chin turret, plus two pods each holding 19 × 2.75in rockets under the stub wings.

A platoon leader scans the terrain ahead as his men cross open ground. There were two styles of using radio-telephone operators. Some leaders did all the talking themselves, and the RTO was really just a radio-bearer. Others relayed what they wanted said, and the RTO did all the talking; such RTOs were on the ball and knew what to do, routinely requesting artillery support or making a situation report without having to be told.

when flights were held in holding patterns over "hot" areas. Attack helicopters (gunships) also provided valuable fire support. A light fire team (a gunship and a light observation helicopter), or a heavy fire team with an additional gunship, provided accurate rocket, machine-gun, and grenade fire.

Fighter-bombers could deliver 500lb, 750lb, and 1,000lb general-purpose and napalm bombs very accurately, but it was essential that friendly positions be precisely marked. Cluster bombs were not used close to friendly troops, because of the wide dispersal of bomblets. Infantrymen could not talk directly to CAS fighter-bombers; coordination was conducted through an airborne forward air controller (FAC) aboard a spotter aircraft. FACs were equipped with radios allowing direct contact with both infantrymen and the fighter-bombers; they would orbit over an assigned area, relaying requests for CAS. When the strike flight arrived on-station the FAC would already have identified the location of the friendly unit, and he then marked the target with WP rockets. He continued to orbit, serving as an air traffic controller to vector the "fast-movers" in and relay corrections from the "ground-pounders."

Normally the CAS could not be brought in as close to friendly positions as artillery, and it was essential that attack runs be made parallel to the unit's long axis, and not overhead or toward it. Helicopter gunships could deliver their comparatively light ordnance much closer to friendly positions. Another advantage was that the infantry could talk directly to the observation helicopter accompanying the gunships, or even to the gunships themselves.

Radio communications

All of this fire support required reliable radio communications, something that could not be guaranteed in Vietnam's rugged terrain. Rifle companies and platoons carried the AN/PRC-25 or -77 radio. The "Prick-25" and the "77" were basically the same radio; the latter used less power, and had a fitting for a secure voice scrambler, and other refinements making it more reliable. This versatile man-packed FM radio was used by all Free World Forces, along with the earlier AN/PRC-10. The "Prick-25" was heavy, at 23.5lbs including battery, and batteries lasted a day or less, depending on how much transmitting was done. When moving, the radio-telephone operator used a 3ft tape antenna with a planning range of 5 miles, but a 10ft "fishing pole" antenna could be fitted for longer range when in static use. Range was actually erratic, as was reception, especially when beneath triple-canopy forest and in the mountains. Radio relay sites were established on hilltops, and helicopters were used as airborne relay stations.

An important point about fire support – whether by artillery, CAS, or helicopter – was that any soldier, regardless of rank, could request and coordinate it. This was a key factor in saving units when casualties among leaders mounted, or when small patrols or outposts made contact.

SMALL-UNIT TACTICS

Linear and non-linear battlefields

The US Army was essentially a general-purpose force capable of worldwide deployment. It was an expeditionary army designed to fight overseas, and in theory its organization, equipment and tactics allowed it to fight anywhere in the world, against any enemy. It maintained forward deployed forces allowing rapid response to regional conflicts – major forces in West Germany and South Korea, prepared to resist conventional invasions, and small forces in Alaska, Panama, Hawaii, and Okinawa. Formations in the States were deployable to any regional contingency mission, but were mainly intended to reinforce forces engaged in Germany and Korea.

The point here is that the primary focus of the US Army and Marines was to be prepared to deploy anywhere in the world and engage what would probably be a superior enemy force on conventional "linear" battlefields.

F: FREE WORLD FORCES AMBUSH TECHNIQUES
The layout adopted by an ambushing force was greatly dependent on terrain, on the enemy's likely route of approach, and his movement formations. The distance of the ambush force from the "kill zone" was governed by the terrain and by density of vegetation. These examples are "near ambushes" – i.e., within grenade-throwing range from concealing vegetation. The security elements of the ambush force might be from two to five men, depending on strength and mission.
F1: The linear ambush was the most basic and common, and for a small force – here, a single squad – it was the only practical formation. Key: **1** = leader, **2** = rear security.
F2: A platoon-strength ambush, including MGs – **3** – allowed more sophistication. Here, more security elements are available – **4 & 5** – critical on the flanks. Claymore mines – **1** – had to be emplaced carefully, at least 16 yards from friendly personnel, but anybody within 100 yards of a Claymore had to be under cover even if behind the mine (the description "directional mine" was relative). Trip-grenades – **2** – took time to set.
F3: The deadly "L"-shaped ambush was the preferred formation, if the terrain would accommodate it. The "short arm" perpendicular to the enemy's path allowed enfilading fire down the enemy formation's long axis, ideally with a machine gun – **3** –, in addition to the flanking fire of the main force forming the "long arm." Here, another MG is positioned to fire on the rear of the enemy column, to engage any enemy outside the kill zone, or any attempting to flee. Care had to be taken to prevent the enfilading fire from raking into the friendly "long arm," so this had to be positioned a safe distance from the kill zone. The ambush leader – **2** – is positioned at the angle of the "L" for maximum control.
F4: The "V"-shaped ambush was rarely used, as it required ideal terrain – a sunken road, a gulley, or – as here – between hillside ridge fingers. It was too easy for the arms of the ambush to fire into one another. Key: **1** = Claymore, **2** = MG.
F5 & F6: Triangular and "X"-shaped ambushes were also little used, but were effective in open areas – large rice paddies, fields, swamps, etc. – where the enemy might approach from any direction, along paddy dikes or a maze of trails. Using dikes for cover, the ambushers would position themselves on opposite sides, and creep over to the appropriate side only when the enemy's approach was identified. Key: **1** = MG, **2** = leader.

F1

F2

F3

F4

F5

F6

An M60 gunner of a platoon passing through an abandoned and destroyed village. Concrete houses such as these had been built by the French for plantation workers, mostly prior to World War II.

They would either reinforce an on-going defense, or conduct a counteroffensive. The enemy would most likely possess superior numbers of aircraft, tanks, and artillery, and the battle might even involve nuclear, biological, and chemical weapons.

Little of this was applicable in Vietnam, which was a "non-linear" battlefield. There were no frontlines, no enemy fixed positions or headquarters, artillery positions, supply dumps, or other targets found on a conventional battlefield. Rather than being assigned relatively narrow defense sectors or attack zones, with a 12- to 18-mile frontage, divisions were given a tactical area of responsibility (TAOR) of 2,000–5,000 square miles. An example of a small TAOR in Vietnam is one of 2,400 square miles, measuring roughly 40 × 60 miles, and most divisions had even larger TAORs.

America's involvement in Vietnam began in 1961, when this was still very much a guerrilla war. Other communist-backed wars of "national liberation" were emerging throughout the world. President John F. Kennedy directed the US armed forces to establish appropriate counterinsurgency forces to combat insurgents, support friendly governments, train their armed forces, and "win the hearts and minds" of the population – the key to successful counterinsurgency.

Specialized units were indeed formed: the Army Special Forces, Navy SEALs, and Air Commandos. Barebones manuals were prepared, addressing counterinsurgencies, guerrilla warfare, and jungle operations. But these manuals only covered the most basic principles, since they had to be applicable to any part of the world – in very varied political, military, and cultural circumstances and conditions of terrain and climate, and against very varied opposing forces. Even though Vietnam was the main conflict, and was forecast to continue for some time, manuals and doctrine could not address that war alone. The Army's 1962 FM 7-20, *Infantry, Airborne Infantry, and Mechanized Infantry Battalions* – the 439-page outline tactical field manual with which it went to war – dedicated only five pages of very broad guidelines to antiguerrilla operations.

A patrol stays alert as they move slowly down a jungle trail. In such vegetation the visibility was limited to a few yards, and hearing was more valuable than sight.

At the height of the war the US Army possessed 19 divisions, and 12 separate brigades and cavalry regiments (the five armored cavalry regiments were equivalent to combined-arms maneuver brigades). Seven of the divisions and three brigades/regiments served in Vietnam, plus two brigades detached from Stateside divisions. Five divisions and three brigades remained in the continental US; seven other divisions were elsewhere overseas, as were six brigades/regiments. Many overseas and Stateside forces were understrength, with the priority for troops going to Vietnam. Of the Marine Corps' four divisions and their 12 infantry regiments, two divisions with eight regiments served in Vietnam. Since the United States had worldwide commitments, troops were not trained specifically for Vietnam, but were given basic conventional infantry training that allowed them to be posted anywhere. Some extremely basic Vietnam-oriented instruction was given during infantry training, but it was within their units that troops were trained for their specific area of operations and mission. Officers were still taught conventional tactics; there was some orientation on counterinsurgency and tactics used in Vietnam, but over all they were versed in conventional warfare.

There were many instances in which gullies and shallow streambeds – as seen here in the background – were used as hasty defensive positions by infantry. Such features would be incorporated into a company's "remain overnight" position.

"Triangular" organization

Since the small-unit tactics used in Vietnam were adapted from conventional doctrine, a basic explanation of the latter is necessary. Infantry were trained and organized to fight on a linear battlefield with an identifiable frontline, but when in the defense there would be gaps between units, with elements deployed to cover avenues of approach. There would be no continuous frontlines, just as there seldom had been in World War II.

Units were organized on a "triangular" basis, with three maneuver subunits plus (usually) a fire support subunit. A division had three maneuver brigades backed by the division artillery, which had four battalions plus attachments. Maneuver brigades normally comprised three maneuver battalions, and battalions could be switched between brigades as necessary for missions.[5] There was no dedicated brigade-level fire support unit other than what was attached from division. The maneuver battalions had three (from 1967, four) rifle or "line" companies, with the fire support elements forming part of the headquarters company until most battalions received a combat support company. Rifle companies had three rifle platoons and a weapons platoon; rifle platoons consisted of three rifle squads and a weapons squad.

Regardless of echelon, these triangular units were deployed "two up, one back" in the attack or defense – i.e., two subunits would be forward to attack or defend, while one was held in reserve. In the attack, the reserve subunit could reinforce success (never reinforce defeat); relieve an exhausted unit to maintain tactical tempo; maneuver to attack the enemy from the flank, or envelop him; protect an exposed flank; or pursue a withdrawing enemy. In the defense, the reserve subunit could reinforce a forward unit under pressure; block an enemy breakthrough; conduct a counterattack; or protect a flank.

Counterinsurgency, in Vietnam or anywhere else, ignores the concept of a linear battlefield. Operations are routinely conducted over wide areas in

---

5. Maneuver battalions were infantry, light infantry, airborne, airmobile, mechanized, and tank. In Vietnam, infantry and light infantry were assigned to infantry divisions, which might also have a mechanized or tank battalion assigned.

rugged terrain, often under harsh climatic conditions. The frontline was literally the direction in which one happened to be facing – the "18-inch front." A static unit, regardless of its size, had to prepare a 360-degree defense, and a moving unit had to be prepared to engage the enemy from any direction. Defensive positions, such as firebases, base camps, and compounds in urban areas, had to be prepared for an all-round defense. Adjacent canals, rivers, swamps, especially dense vegetation, and the proximity of villages were no guarantee that an attack would not come from that direction.

PATROLS

Patrols were important in counterinsurgency operations, and even more so in close terrain where visibility was so limited and the enemy so mobile. Basically there were three types of patrols: reconnaissance, security, and combat. Size, composition, and armament depended on the mission. Patrols were typically of short duration – a few hours, overnight, or a few days at the most. This allowed patrols to travel light, or to carry more weapons and ammunition instead of subsistence supplies.

Free World battalions had a reconnaissance platoon that normally operated as a single unit, but in some instances sent out squad- or team-sized patrols, and might temporarily be attached to rifle companies. ARVN battalions did not have reconnaissance platoons; from 1966 high-priority regiments received a reconnaissance company, but these often operated as a strike unit. Separate brigades had a company-sized, vehicle-mounted reconnaissance unit, while divisions had a similar battalion-sized unit. The different countries' units operated very differently. Some operated afoot, in both large and small elements; others were mounted on tracked vehicles, and some – particularly US armored cavalry squadrons – had helicopter capabilities. Separate brigades and divisions also possessed long-range patrol companies employing teams of four to eight men. Regardless of dedicated reconnaissance units, most patrols were conducted by elements of rifle

A hastily cleared firebase atop a hill; these were often partially cleared by first blasting the hilltop with heavy artillery and air strikes. They were usually temporary, housing only a 105mm howitzer battery to support an operation, with a rifle company for defense. A CH-47 Chinook cargo helicopter can just be seen in the center.

Many firebases and other installations could only be supplied by helicopter. Here rations are being rigged in cargo nets to be sling-loaded beneath CH-47 Chinooks.

companies. Patrols of all types were just as much part of a rifle platoon's roles as offense and defense.

Platoons and squads would modify their organization for a patrol, depending entirely on the patrol's size and mission. Sometimes patrols might be assembled using selected personnel from within a platoon, and tactical organization was ignored. Besides the patrol leader, an assistant patrol leader was designated, who typically brought up the rear, ensuring that nobody got separated or left behind after halts. If the patrol was ambushed, it was usually the assistant leader who organized the counterattack, if he was outside the kill zone. The patrol leader was positioned near the head of the main body, close enough to the point to direct his patrol's actions if engaged, but not so far forward as to be exposed among the point element. The point consisted of more than just the pointman. He was responsible for his immediate front, searching for booby traps, mines, and any sign of the enemy; he had to be extremely focused, and could not be distracted by other duties. One or two men were close behind him, tasked with looking further ahead and to their immediate flanks. One man near the point was the navigator, who kept the patrol on course, estimating their location on the map and the distance traveled. The pointman – or for that matter, any man in the patrol – had the authority to signal the patrol to halt, take cover, or take other preventive action.

Depending on the mission, specialists might accompany patrols. These might include artillery/mortar forward observers, snipers, demolition specialists, combat engineers for bridge or terrain reconnaissance, scout dogs to detect the presence of the enemy, interpreters, local guides from militia units, Vietnamese police to make arrests, and Kit Carson scouts ("turned" NVA/VC who defected to Free World Forces). Such attachments were not too common, and were often considered a hindrance; many troops did not like working with outsiders of unknown quality or reliability who might not pull their weight.

Reconnaissance patrols were usually small, comprising a squad or a team, but might be of up to platoon strength. By definition, reconnaissance patrols avoided contact with the enemy if at all possible. They would move quietly, through difficult terrain where they were less likely to encounter enemy patrols or civilians. While avoiding heavier weapons, reconnaissance patrols were as well armed as a combat patrol, in case they were engaged by the enemy; if so, they would have to fight their way out, or hold out for extraction or relief by a larger force. Their mission was to locate the enemy by spotting signs of his presence and plotting trails, and to report terrain conditions to the parent unit. They sometimes conducted bomb (or battle) damage-assessment (BDA) missions, reporting enemy casualties and damage. They also determined if the enemy remained in the area, and might call for subsequent artillery or air strikes.

The ideal reconnaissance patrol would not only avoid detection by the enemy, but would leave no signs to let the enemy know they had been there. There were exceptions, however. The nature of the war was such that engaging the enemy was the desired goal, and opportunities to inflict casualties might be rare – the aim of Free World operations, after all, was to kill as many of the enemy as possible, to make the war too costly for him to pursue. It was therefore not uncommon for platoon-sized reconnaissance patrols to be tasked with both locating and engaging the enemy, whereupon reinforcements would be helicoptered or marched in. Often units would conduct saturation patrols, in which numerous small patrols would infiltrate into an area by foot or be inserted by helicopter in an effort to locate enemy elements quickly, when they would call for a standby reaction force to be helicopter-inserted. The enemy might strive to disengage, or might choose to escalate the action and turn it into a pitched battle. Division-size battles sometimes resulted from a simple chance encounter between small opposing patrols.

B-rations are served on paper plates while a firebase is cleared. The blasted bare patch and the shattered bamboo indicate that at least 500lb bombs have been used to blast a clearing.

A reconnaissance patrol might be organized into one or more reconnaissance teams to reconnoiter one or more sites. For an area reconnaissance, the patrol might be broken into smaller patrols to sweep the area. While an objective was being reconnoitered, they might put out one or more security teams to protect approaches from different directions.

Security patrols were typically of squad or team size, but larger patrols were employed if enemy activity was heavy. Security patrols were conducted around firebases, base camps, and larger installations. Their goal was to detect enemy activity on the approaches to bases. They looked for trails, discarded equipment, signs of the preparation of firing positions, and so on.

Combat patrols looked for trouble; the Australians used the British term "fighting patrols." They might be of platoon size, but company-size were common; besides the greater rifle strength, these allowed for the necessary additional security, blocking, and fire support elements (see Plate E). Combat patrols needed to be sufficiently strong to fight their way out of engagements with larger-than-expected forces. They normally had a specific objective, or a small area in which they searched for a suspected enemy. They were actually a form of raid – a surprise attack on an enemy position to kill and capture personnel, destroy and capture weapons, equipment, and supplies, and disrupt operations, before departing the area immediately. Combat patrols were also dispatched to recover Free World dead from engagement or aircraft crash sites, or to recover weapons, radios, equipment, and documents from downed aircraft and abandoned battle-damaged vehicles. Combat patrols also cleared roads for vehicle traffic, checking for mines, booby traps, and command-detonated mine firing wires. Combat patrols might retain the subunit's normal tactical organization, but might be divided into an assault element, a fire support element, and a security element. The assault element might be further broken down into search, recovery, or capture teams.

The missions of patrols often overlapped. A large combat patrol could dispatch smaller patrols to reconnoiter routes or to detect enemy elements. A reconnaissance patrol might attack a small enemy element as a target of opportunity, or it might establish a patrol base and send out a security patrol to check on the surrounding area.

AMBUSHES

While all ambushes sought to inflict casualties on the enemy from concealment, they varied greatly in size and intentions. Free World Forces used them as a security measure around bases, establishing squad- and platoon-sized ambushes on likely approaches in hopes of catching enemy patrols or forces moving into attack positions. Units operating in the field might set ambushes on nearby trails during lengthy rest halts. At night they might do the same in order to protect themselves from surprise attacks.

G COUNTERAMBUSH

Reacting effectively to an ambush was always chancy; reaction drills had to be fast and flexible, and only trained forces with experienced leaders had any chance of, at best, avoiding heavy casualties. The reaction – especially to a close-range ambush – had to be immediate and violent, making maximum use of firepower to break out of or withdraw from the kill zone, gain fire superiority, and counterattack the ambushers, but this was very difficult to achieve. Small-scale NVA/VC ambushes were similar to Free World practice, usually being linear or "L"-shaped. However, enemy ambushes were often large, elaborate, and well-planned, especially those intended to catch a convoy, or reinforcements coming to the aid of a base under attack or a previously ambushed force. The few counterambush drills that were specified in manuals were simplistic, and failed to address the complex techniques developed during the French Indochina War of 1946–54.

G1: This depicts a counterambush technique used by some units, here a platoon. A point squad moved well ahead of the main body, giving the impression that it was alone. This "bait" squad was well armed; its task was admittedly dangerous, but no more so than if the whole platoon was ambushed together. A machine gun accompanied the second squad, along with two grenadiers, allowing it to immediately support the bait squad; the other machine gun accompanied the third squad. The second squad might support the lead squad with its heavy firepower, or maneuver to outflank the ambushers alongside the third squad. This technique only worked if moving on a trail, or in moderate vegetation; otherwise the main body could lose contact with the fairly distant lead squad. *Key:* **1** = Plt leader, **2** = RTO, **3** = Plt sgt, **4** = MG, **5** = grenadier.

G2: This demonstrates how the NVA/VC attempted – often successfully – to anticipate counterambush reactions. In this scenario two truck-mounted ARVN companies, on their way (predictably) to relieve a fortified village under enemy attack, have been ambushed and pinned down – **1**. The ambushers typically attempted to destroy the lead and rear vehicles first, thus trapping the others in the kill zone. The convoy's rearguard, outside the kill zone, have dismounted to counterattack – **2**; but the ambushers have anticipated this, deploying a blocking platoon to frustrate them – **3**. In expectation of the dispatch of a relief force, a second, smaller ambush has been set for it, far enough down the road to prevent the two ARVN elements from supporting one another – **4** & **5**. Knowing there is a possibility of airmobile reinforcement, the enemy commander has also deployed Local Force squads – **6** – at the two LZs in the area, to harass the landing helicopters and to warn the Main Force element. Helicopters could use the wide Rome-plowed road as an LZ, but had to land a considerable distance from the action. The VC commander has also designated a reserve – **7** – to meet any force airlifted in, or to handle any other unexpected developments. It is easy to see how such ambushes could escalate into large actions, as more and more forces were committed by both sides.

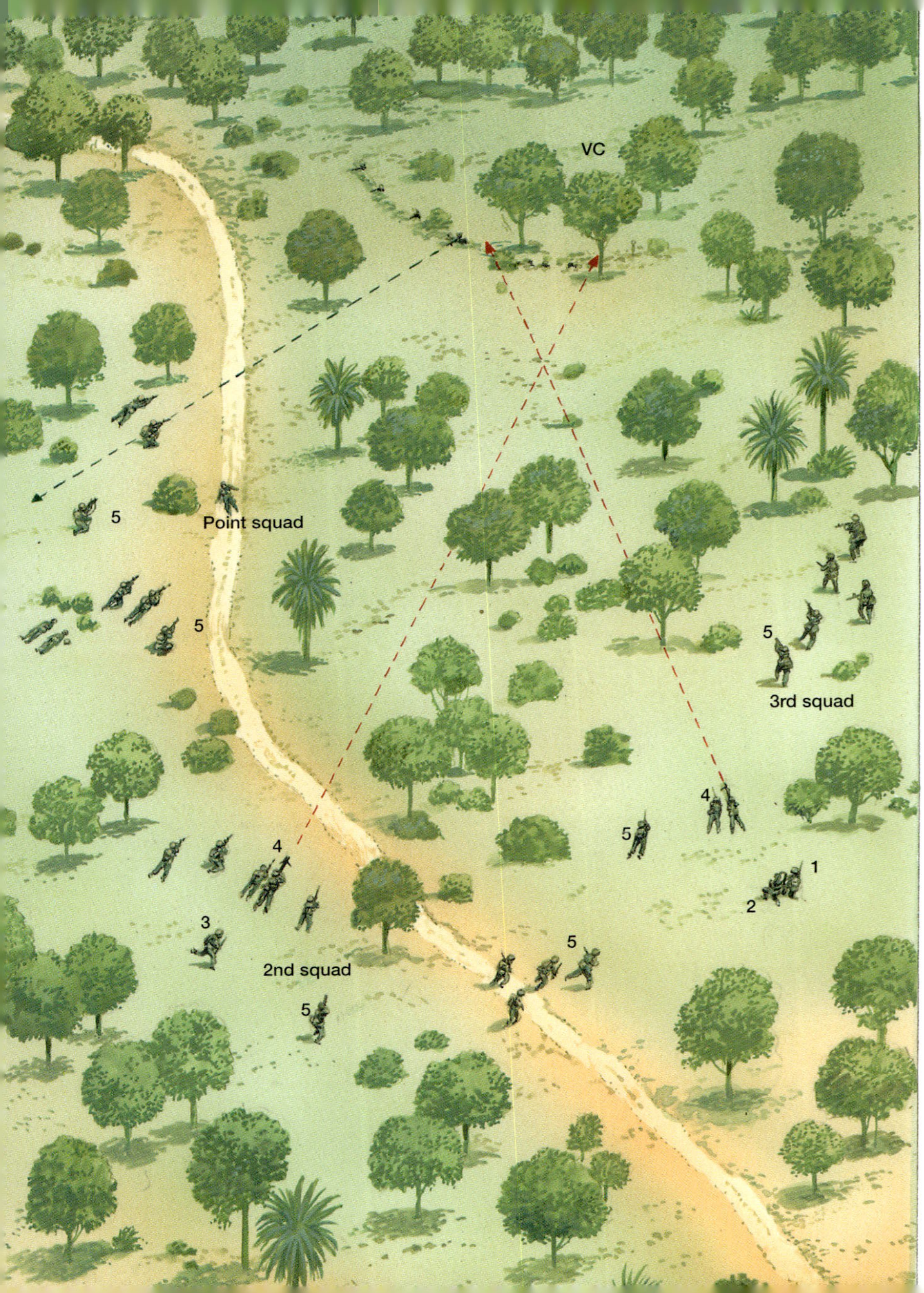
VC
5
Point squad
5
5
3rd squad
4
5
4
1
2
3
2nd squad
5
5

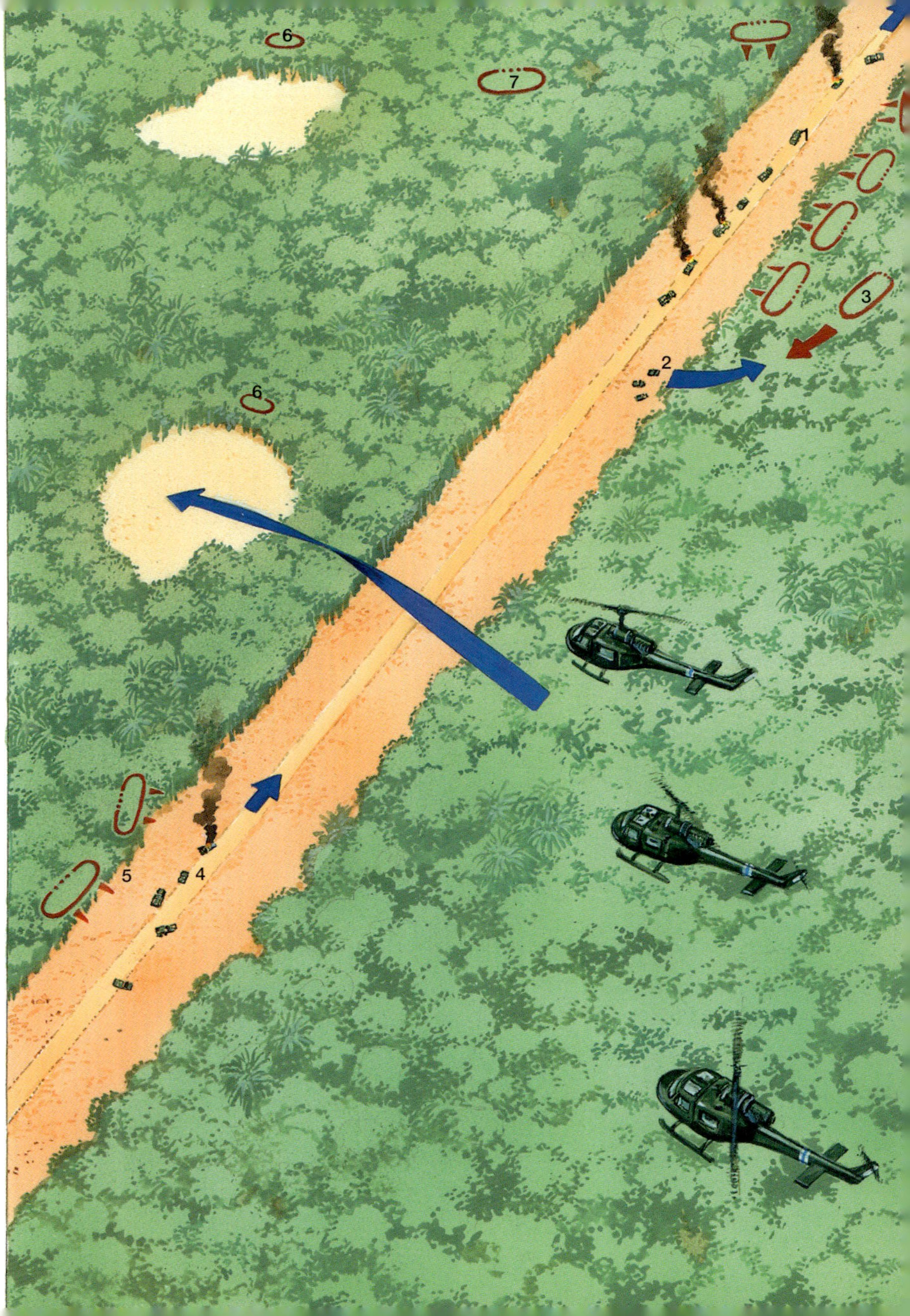
6
7
1
3
2
6
5
4

Another technique was for a company to quietly move into an area, and set platoon- or even squad-size ambushes on enemy routes that reconnaissance patrols had previously determined to be in use. Such ambushes might be set up on trails, roads leading into villages, stream crossings, water points, and canals and rivers bearing enemy traffic. Ambushes were usually established for the night and early morning hours when the enemy was most active.

A properly organized ambush would consist of the assault force, that would cover the "kill zone"; the support element, including crew-served weapons (machine guns, recoilless rifles, LAWs); and the security element. The latter could comprise several teams. One would be placed on either flank to warn of the enemy's approach, to engage anyone fleeing from the kill zone, and to protect the ambush force's flanks. Another security team would protect the rally point, where rucksacks would be left. Depending on the plan, one team of the assault element would be designated to enter the kill zone after the action, to recover weapons, equipment, and materials of intelligence value.

Most ambushes were planned or deliberate, but hasty ambushes were also practiced. This was when a unit unexpectedly encountered a moving enemy force, and was able to move into an ambush position undetected. This was simply a form of "meeting engagement," when two moving units collided; the outcome depended on who detected whom first.

There was no "typical" ambush, since techniques varied from unit to unit, and everything depended on the terrain and local enemy situation. Much emphasis has been placed on the layout or shape of the ambush force – sometimes too much emphasis. An Australian assessment of their ambushes noted that one battalion commander was adamant that irrespective of the ground, an "L"-shaped ambush was always best. In fact the layout needed to be adapted to the terrain, the available weapons, and the direction of the enemy's approach, as well as his known counterambush drills (see Plate F).

The most common layout was the "linear ambush," in which the ambush force simply lined up parallel with the enemy's route, usually on a trail, road, or canal. Another common layout was the "L-shaped ambush" – a linear ambush with a shorter "arm" at 90 degrees to the main firing line. This arm blocked the enemy column's route of travel, and could add devastating enfilading fire down the column's long axis to the flanking fire delivered all along it by the main firing line. A "V-shaped ambush" was normally set up on both sides of a route running through a draw (gulley), sunken road, or other depression, but this was dangerous, since the two arms might fire into each other if the fire was not completely directed downward. There were also "triangle ambushes," "X-shaped ambushes," and "pinwheel ambushes." These odd formations might occasionally be used in open areas, such as among rice paddies, where the ambushers were dug in atop or behind dikes and arrayed in a manner to engage an enemy approaching from any direction. The triangular was the most common of these; it was the easiest to control,

Infantrymen at a firebase assemble before heading out for one of the local security patrols that were necessary to protect such positions. They would leave behind their rucksacks and carry belt gear only, but note the armor vests. In the background is a battery of 155mm M114A1 howitzers.

and offered less danger of the ambushers firing into each other.

Getting into position
The occupation of ambush positions was a critical phase. This had to be accomplished undetected, not only by enemy combatants but also by civilians. Ideally the site would be reconnoitered in advance to find the best position, study the terrain (to include on the far side of the kill zone), and determine withdrawal routes.

Ruses were used to disguise the establishment of an ambush. An ambush force might be dropped off surreptitiously during an apparent rest halt by a mechanized unit moving through the area. A company moving on foot might have the ambush force dispersed through its formation, with individuals dropping off at designated points and then moving to the ambush site, sometimes after dark. Another method was for the ambush force to split off from a main body and circle back to ambush its back-trail or another location.

When the site was reached, security had to be established while Claymores and other traps were installed and the positions were occupied and camouflaged. Likely escape routes, to include either direction on the enemy's movement route, and dense vegetation, ditches, and gullies, had to be covered by Claymores, trip-wired grenades, or small teams. Command-detonated demolition charges were sometime buried alongside the route to stun and kill.

There was more to an ambush than simply occupying a suitable position and waiting for an unsuspecting enemy. Noise discipline was essential; men had to refrain from coughing, talking, movement, and making noise with their equipment – even the click of setting selector levers on weapons. Patience was critical – and this was not a characteristic typical of Western troops.

A battalion commander discusses an operation with two of his company commanders. Regardless of the ability to transmit orders by radio, face-to-face coordination was important. It allowed the commander to more effectively express his concepts, and assess the state of his subordinates.

Ranges
There is a mistaken impression that ambushes were set up "right on top" of the enemy's anticipated route. In some situations, especially in extremely dense vegetation, this was unavoidable, but ideally the force would be set up at a longer range. This allowed each shooter a wider field of fire to engage more targets; provided standoff protection from the ambush's own Claymores, M79s, grenades, etc., and placed the ambushers out of enemy grenade range – i.e. about 25 yards. A close-up ambush, besides placing the ambush force within enemy grenade range, allowed the enemy the chance to simply rush the force while firing, pass through, and disperse into the vegetation. Longer range allowed sufficient time, while the enemy was charging, to destroy such attempts to break through the ambush force.

Counterambush tactics
Generally, this is exactly what ambushed troops – NVA/VC or Free World – would attempt to do, since to remain in the kill zone at close range was suicidal. In a longer-range ambush, i.e. at least beyond grenade range, those caught in the kill zone took cover and returned fire, while any outside the

An infantry unit, well dispersed as they cross a field in the background, is funneled onto a wide dike between rice paddies. In areas that were being actively worked by farmers such trails were seldom booby-trapped.

kill zone immediately assaulted the ambushers, preferably "rolling up" a flank (see Plate C3.) Ideally, such a flanking attack would distract the ambushers and force them to shift fires to meet the threat; they might even be forced to reposition men and reduce the fire into the kill zone, allowing those trapped there to maneuver. The counterattack might even force the

H "REMAIN OVERNIGHT" POSITION

Any unit coiling up for the night, whether a company or battalion, assumed a similar pattern of positions. These were usually three- or four-sided, or sometimes circular, but depending upon terrain and vegetation they might be more irregular in shape. RON occupation procedures varied widely. Some units cut an LZ with chainsaws, hacked out fields of fire, and constructed hasty sandbagged bunkers; this was, of course, extremely noisy, and pinpointed their position. Other units reconnoitered a position discreetly, and moved quietly into it only after darkness fell, maintaining strict noise and light discipline. In such cases the NVA/VC might not even be able to locate it, or would at least be unable to determine its layout.

H1: One method of occupying a RON was for a company to pass through the area, assigning sectors to each platoon. The platoons then separated, with one remaining behind as the base platoon, while the other two moved further on and then split left and right, to angle back on the flanks of the base platoon. The platoon leader and sergeant would "dress up" the perimeter to ensure there were no gaps; the platoon leader would designate the machine-gun positions, and the squad leaders would designate positions for each pair of men.

H2: Another method was for the company CO and platoon leaders and sergeants to assemble at the center of the future perimeter. The platoon sergeants would be sent out to mark the flanks for each platoon, and the platoon leaders would then lead the men into their sectors, using the platoon sergeants as guides to anchor their flanks.

H3: Such neat "geometric" positions were used in, for example, a forest or plantation. In other terrain, with irregular features, clumps of trees and brush, the perimeter would be determined by the particular ground. Each platoon or company might not necessarily be assigned an equally wide sector of the defenses. For example, if one side of the perimeter faced rice paddies then that platoon might be given a wide sector, while the others, facing more dangerous ground concealed by brush, had shorter sectors. *Key:* **1** = leader, **2** = mortar squad, **3** = subunit leader, **4** = MG.

H4: Typically, a platoon had 13–17 two-man positions, 10–20 yards apart. The two-man holes would be dug about 2ft deep, with the spoil piled up to the front, to provide kneeling firing positions. Throughout the night, one of each pair of men was supposed to remain alert, on two-hour shifts.

H5: Meanwhile, his buddy tried to get some sleep in a shallow slit trench dug long enough for him to lie prone, about 10–20 yards to the rear of the fighting position.

Each platoon would reconnoiter for a short distance to their front before locking down for the night. Each squad would emplace two or three Claymores and 10–15 trip flares, to be recovered in the morning.

H1

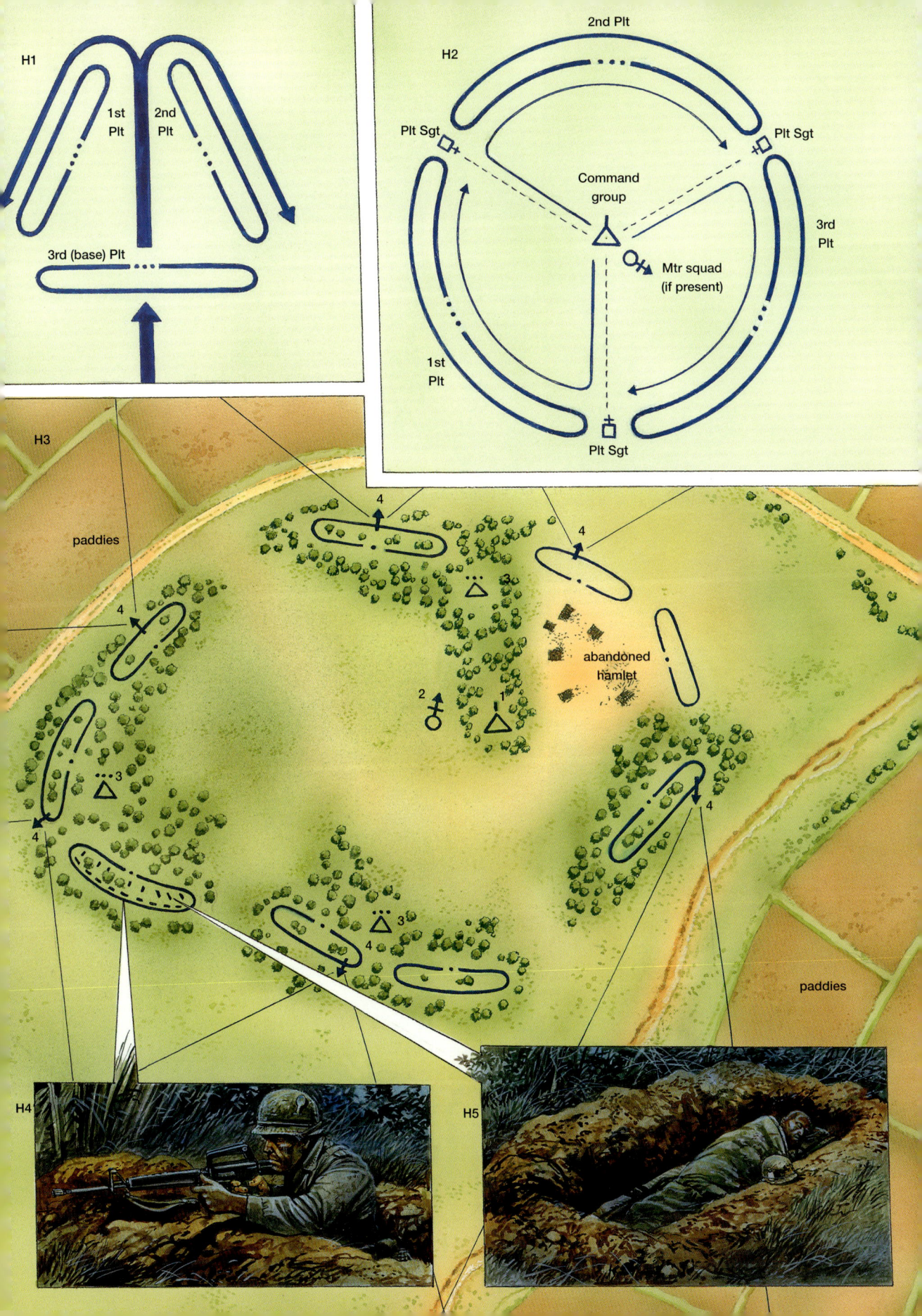

1st Plt   2nd Plt

3rd (base) Plt

H2

2nd Plt

Plt Sgt   Plt Sgt

Command group

3rd Plt

Mtr squad (if present)

1st Plt

Plt Sgt

H3

paddies

abandoned hamlet

paddies

H4

H5

A rifle platoon leader orients his map to the terrain. Under magnification, the cross marked on the map can be seen to be designated DEAN. This is a location reference identifier; the unit's location would be reported according to the distance from the cross in kilometers – for example, "2.5 up and 3.3 right" (2,500m north and 3,300m east). To confuse enemy monitors even more, such a reference might be identified as e.g. CAT, but each time the unit reported its location it would call it by the name of a different sort of cat – for example, "TABBY, 3.4 down, 1.8 left."

ambushers to withdraw. Regardless, however, any force caught in an even moderately well-planned kill zone would suffer heavy punishment (see Plate G).

Whether on foot or mounted, a Free World force moving on a road deployed tactically, dispersed with wide intervals between vehicles and subunits. An advance guard preceded the main body by no more than three minutes, flank security was deployed (though this was not always possible), and a well-armed rear guard followed. The commander was positioned well forward, but not with the point. For motorized columns, armed and armored escort vehicles were distributed through the convoy. Ambushes could be defeated, but it was much more desirable to employ effective tactics and techniques to counter them before they were initiated.

Typical errors

A poor signal to initiate the ambush might cause failure. The signal could be given by firing an automatic weapon, LAW, or Claymore mines. An M79 grenade-launcher was inadequate, since the faint pop of its firing might not be heard by all of the ambush force, while it might alert the enemy, and the round's detonation would be too late. If the commander initiated the ambush by firing his weapon, he needed to shouted "Fire!" loudly in case the weapon misfired. Initiating the ambush too early, before most of the enemy were within the kill zone, was a classic mistake. Ideally, the other side of the kill zone should have been sown with tripwire-activated grenades, Claymores, or punji stakes; but this was seldom done, as it was time-consuming, and might leave signs that warned the enemy.

Insufficient firepower was sometimes placed in the kill zone. This was usually due to an inexperienced leader underestimating just how much firepower was necessary to devastate the enemy. Another error was failure to pursue the enemy by fire even after he had disappeared from view; automatic weapons should have continued to fire into the direction of withdrawal, keeping the fire low. Likewise, supporting mortars, artillery, and gunships were often not employed to pursue by fire. Sometimes inexperienced leaders failed to prepare for an organized search of the kill zone; individuals needed to be designated for this task – to search enemy casualties, take prisoners, and recover weapons, equipment, and documents for intelligence purposes. The rest of the ambush force needed to be alerted that the search team would be entering the kill zone, so as to both hold their fire, and be ready to cover them from attack by survivors from any direction.

* * *

Once all tasks were accomplished, the ambush force treated friendly casualties, recovered their rucksacks from the rally point, accounted for all personnel, and withdrew, taking precautions to ensure they were not followed. The manpower necessary for such an ambush was normally at least a platoon. However, ambushes – albeit not so elaborate – were also sometimes conducted by teams of four to six men, or by dozen-strong squads. These were usually security-type ambushes established outside firebases, protected villages, or larger halted units; their purpose was simply to engage the enemy, to delay or divert him and warn of his advance. The ambush force would then immediately withdraw – this was purely a hit-and-run attack.

AREA SATURATION OPERATIONS

In 1963, when the 2d ARVN Infantry Division and its US Advisory Team 2 were operating in Quang Ngai and Binh Dinh provinces of southern I CTZ, it was decided that a more effective method of locating and engaging the VC was needed. Battalions were typically assigned areas of operations, and their companies areas within this. Once a company had cleared part of its AO and moved on, the VC tended to simply move into the "cleared" area. The boundaries between unit AOs were not being searched, and the VC used these as corridors to move back into already-searched areas. These fix-and-destroy operations – essentially, shows of force – saw an ARVN unit move into an area and sweep through it searching for the VC, focusing on the small hamlets dotted across the Vietnamese countryside. Such sweeps were largely ineffectual; the VC would simply move out of the way, harass the ARVN with snipers and booby traps, and sometimes mass for hit-and-run attacks.

A C-ration lunch break in the field. US troops often demonstrated poor litter discipline, discarding all manner of trash, damaged gear and clothing, expended batteries, and more. Much of this was of use to the VC, and they would collect such materials after a unit moved on.

A Vietnamese interpreter questions civilians about VC activity in the area. Many units ignored intelligence gained this way, but an experienced leader with a good interpreter could often make an effective assessment of the information, and act on it successfully – while naturally treating it with caution.

To counter this, the division's regiments now placed two battalions in the field with adjacent AOs, while the third battalion provided base security and reaction forces. The AOs did not abut one another – there were gaps between them, to lessen the danger of "friendly fire" contacts – but the intervals between the battalions were covered by harassing and interdiction (H&I) fires. After moving into their zones of action, the battalions would begin saturation patrolling. After about a week the battalions would move into new zones, which overlapped both battalions' former zones and some of the previous intervals between them, and would conduct another week of operations. If enemy movements were significant, a platoon would be loaded in helicopters and operated as an "eagle flight," being directed by aerial observers to intercept, block, or pursue a fleeing enemy element.

Two of a battalion's companies would be assigned AOs, again with gaps between them. The areas were selected based on the terrain and assessment of enemy activity, and might cover anything between about 3 and 19 square miles (obviously, smaller areas were searched more effectively). A third company would be held as a reaction force at the battalion CP, where a mortar platoon was located; the mortars and nearby firebases would provide H&I fires in the intervals between the AOs, as well as supporting fires. Each company would establish a base, from which its platoons would operate and draw resupply every few days. Like the battalions, the companies would periodically shift AOs, which would overlap previously searched AOs and adjacent intervals. Moving by foot to their new AOs also contributed to the area searched.

The battalion base would be switched periodically; if it stayed in one location too long it would invite attack. If there was a hamlet in the area, the battalion might locate there to segregate the population from the enemy.

Local Self-Defense Corps and Civil Guard platoons and companies protecting hamlets would be incorporated into the operation (the LSD and CG became the Popular Forces and Regional Forces, respectively, in 1964 – see MAA 458.) Saturation operations became more effective when battalions later received a fourth company, allowing three companies to conduct saturation patrolling while the fourth provided a reaction force.

The platoons would conduct day and, in some instances, night patrols, but more commonly they established night ambushes to catch the VC when they moved. Even the reaction company would conduct patrols and ambushes close to its base, to cover more ground. The patrols would travel light, leaving behind all unnecessary equipment, packs, helmets, and excess ammunition, and would eat rice balls and canned fish which did not require cooking. Patrol planning was decentralized. The battalion assigned the company AOs and the time allotted before changing AOs, and provided resupply instructions, but the companies selected the routes for their platoons' patrols and their ambush sites. Helicopter surveillance would be conducted over the area at least part of the time. In addition to the ARVN patrolling, ambushing, H&I fires, and deploying reaction forces, civic action teams would visit local hamlets to provide political lectures, medical care, building materials, and agricultural goods, in attempts to win "hearts and minds."

Saturation operations were adopted by US units, and proved effective – much more so than conducting simple, lumbering sweeps through an area. ("Sweeps" were described as moving quickly through an area without diligent search, and were not as productive, since the enemy sidestepped such operations. Maintaining observation over Free World Forces using local guerrillas, they either avoided contact, or awaited opportunities to strike Free World patrols and other small elements.) There were many variations on the saturation theme, adapted to the terrain, enemy situation, available resources, cooperation of local civilians, and commanders' preferences. A constant, however, was that if decentralized operations were to be effective, much depended on the proficiency and aggressiveness of small-unit leaders.

Cordon and search

Cordon-and-search operations were important in the counterinsurgency. The goal was to quickly isolate a village or hamlet, to trap local VC guerrillas and infrastructure – the VC shadow government. (Villages comprised two or more hamlets spread over a small area.) Caches of arms, ammunition, supplies, and documents were also sought. Local VC often lived in the villages rather than occupying remote base camps like the Main Force units. To be effective, these operations were jointly conducted, involving ARVN troops, local Regional and Popular Force militia, and the National Police. (As villages

Contrary to what is often supposed, many civilians in VC-controlled areas willingly assisted Free World Forces. The VC demanded that they provide large amounts of food, and made them fabricate and emplace booby traps, and salvage discarded materials from abandoned firebases. Villagers were pressed into service as lookouts and laborers, and the VC drafted their sons into its ranks. Despite their natural resentment of the RVN government – which was often neglectful, at best – and of foreign soldiers, villagers wanted above all to be left alone. Informing on the VC often seemed the way to ensure this (although it could bring down savage reprisals after the soldiers had left).

A rifleman searches beneath a large fallen tree for a VC hide. The enemy could be very creative in selecting hiding places for men and supplies, and uncovering them demanded meticulous searches.

were to be entered and civilians interrogated, the employment of Western troops was less than ideal. However, the ARVN often ill-treated their own people owing to suspicions of VC support; this occurred on many occasions, usually with Vietnamese militia and police participating, and seriously compromised the "hearts and minds" program.)

It was essential that such operations be planned and executed in secrecy to prevent the targeted community from being warned in time for the VC to escape. The objective and the surrounding area had to be closely reconnoitered to determine the positioning of the cordon and road/trail blocks. Timing was critical, and all the cordon forces needed to be in position at the same time to prevent escape gaps. They would approach from different directions by foot, and usually over long distances. Trucks could be heard at night from a considerable distance away, and their use was therefore limited to moving troops to a distant forward rendezvous, with traffic control.

Ideally, military units would establish the cordon while police, backed by local militiamen familiar with the civilian population, conducted the search of the village and screened villagers; there was a danger that an overly aggressive military search might aggravate the villagers and win further support for the enemy. Although placing a continuous line of troops around a hamlet was neither possible nor necessary, cordons demanded a good many men. The numbers required for an effective cordon naturally varied with the surrounding vegetation and terrain; there were often open rice paddies and cultivated fields around hamlets, and this helped.

The cordon was usually established before dawn. Moving into positions in unfamiliar territory in the dark and while trying to maintain silence was time-consuming, and it was difficult to ensure that no gaps developed. The danger of friendly-fire incidents was high, especially once the search force moved into the hamlet. The cordon had to be established in depth; for example, a platoon would place two squads forward (facing the village) and one squad to the rear, and spread out in two-man teams to catch evaders. An outer cordon was also established, with more widely spread teams deployed some distance from the inner cordon to cover approach and exit routes, to include densely overgrown areas that offered concealed access. Roadblocks were placed on roads and trails entering the hamlet.

If the operation went as planned, the first the villagers knew of the cordon was when police entered from different directions, announcing that the hamlet was surrounded and ordering that all persons turn out into the square or remain in their homes. The headman and other notables were located and questioned. Search parties composed of police and militiamen searched all buildings and areas that might contain caches, or camouflaged entrances to tunnels and hides. Screening teams questioned villagers and checked identity cards, while escort teams led suspects to the "cage" – either a designated hut, or simply an open area where they squatted under guard. Civic action teams might be employed to provide medical and other assistance to the villagers. A reserve was held outside the cordoned area to meet any external attack, attempted breakout, or resistance within the village. Additional truck-mounted and possibly helicopter-delivered reserves might be held further away.

A comrade grips the hand of a "tunnel rat" as he lowers himself into the depths of a VC tunnel. Most tunnel systems were small, just sufficient to hide a few village-defense guerrillas and their weapons.

These operations could be in anything from company to multiple-battalion strength, as some were intended to cordon off large areas containing several villages. Besides military and police forces, a considerable number of militia and elements of various RVN government agencies were involved. There were occasions – as with other types of operation – when cordon and search operations escalated into major battles.

Search and destroy

So much use was made of the phrase "search and destroy" operations by the media that it was later changed to "search and clear." These were usually brigade/regiment, division, or even multiple-division operations, in which forces were inserted into an AO with the mission to search out the enemy, destroy him, and withdraw soon afterward. Heavy use was made of helicopters to insert, supply, and provide the ground force with reconnaissance and fire support, as well as carrying out medical evacuation, relocating forces within the AO, and finally withdrawing them. Such operations might last anything from a couple of weeks to months. While some efforts might be made to provide aid to local civilians during the course of the operation, afterward they were essentially abandoned to the enemy, who would invariably re-establish control in the area after the operation concluded. Other Free World Forces would eventually have to re-enter the area, and bring the enemy to battle once again.

The strategy was often condemned, as it yielded only short-term results. It could achieve little more than temporarily wearing down enemy strength, and the hope of winning a "war of attrition" in Vietnam was futile to begin with. The alternative concept, of "clear and secure" (aka "clear and hold") operations, could only be applied in high-value areas containing agricultural resources and established populations. They would require significant resources, not only in manpower to secure the cleared areas in the long term, but in RVN government services that would have to be introduced. It was not worth the effort to try to clear and hold vast regions of wilderness with sparse populations and only subsistence farming, and there simply were not enough Free World battalions to secure them – thus the doctrine of search and destroy.

Search-and-destroy operations often resulted in villages being burned, crops being destroyed, and the populations being forcibly relocated to secure areas or "strategic hamlets." The goal was to deny the VC a recruiting and labor base, secure base areas, and agricultural produce, but the practice was severely damaging to the morale and livelihood of Vietnamese rural populations. An additional aim was to keep the enemy on the move and dispersed – to prevent him from assembling, planning, and executing operations on his own initiative, or simply to deny him undisturbed training time. Most of these operations were conducted without detailed prior information on the enemy. Commanders had to develop their own intelligence, as well as receiving intelligence from external sources as the operation developed.

Regardless of the large scale of search-and-destroy operations, within their overall scope the small-unit tactics and techniques employed involved all manner of sweeps, patrols, ambushes, and other minor small-scale activity.

A Vietnamese interpreter interrogates a wounded VC. It was often found that such information was good, and helped a great deal in further operations. Key questions included the location of the VC unit's base, its strength, weapons, future intentions and movement, and morale.

CONCLUSIONS

Vietnam did not significantly change the doctrine of how the US Army and Marines fought conventional wars, but it did have an impact. Many techniques were adopted that applied just as well to conventional warfare as to unconventional warfare in the jungle: operations and movement on rugged terrain with limited visibility; patrolling, ambush and counterambush; weapons-employment techniques; close combat using AFVs; direction of supporting fires, communications, and airmobile operations. These techniques were often incorporated into field manual revisions. Aviation and airmobile operations were now fully integrated into operations, and aviation units were much expanded, to the point that Army Aviation became a separate combat branch in 1983.

The most significant change was in individual and small-unit tactics and procedures. The many precise skills learned in patrolling, ambushing, and maneuvering small units resulted in their being formalized in manuals. In the mid-1970s, new squad and platoon movement formations were introduced based on the lessons learned in Vietnam, combined with the "battle drill" concept used so successfully by the Australians and New Zealanders. The